dedication

To William, born with the PC and now fully equipped and upgraded.

acknowledgments

This book has a single name on the cover, but represents the hard work of dozens of professionals worthy of appreciation.

Thanks to Michael Sprague at McGraw-Hill for continuing our publishing relationship into a second generation. The editorial and production staff at McGraw-Hill polished my words and made them look good on paper.

Thanks, too, to photographer Jack Weinhold, master of the completely digital photo studio for this project.

My longtime cohort Tom Badgett pitched in with technical support and good humor, both of which are always prized. And as always, Janice Keefe ran the office and the author with efficiency and love.

Have you ever wished you could run twice as fast? How about being able to lift much more weight, have the best intellect of your generation, and acquire the skills of an engineer and the eye of an artist? And while you're at it, why not do it all with movie star looks?

Even in this day of plastic surgery and miracle drugs, there's only so much you can do to change yourself. Your body, as produced by the original equipment manufacturer (remember mommy?), had its basic specifications and limitations preset before delivery. This is not the case with modern computers.

Consider the PC as an electronic train set. You can change track, add sections, install new engines and cars, and even improve the bells and whistles.

Or perhaps you'd rather think in terms of working on your car. You can change the tires, upgrade components of the engine, or even swap the old motor for a new and improved one.

Today's computers are modular constructions, built from blocks that can be easily moved around or replaced. That's not to say that every change or upgrade makes technical or economic sense. In this book, we explore the options and help you decide whether upgrades are worth the effort and cost.

PC Economics

However you think of the upgrade process—as a train set, automobile, or a stack of blocks—the most important first step in considering an upgrade is to figure out what is possible and what makes sense.

The good news about personal computers is that they continue to become faster and more capable as their relative or actual price goes down. In recent years, the magic price for a machine that meets the needs of most home and business users has hovered in the range between about $1,000 and $1,200.

The bad news is that, if you purchase each of the individual parts of that machine, you're almost certain to spend more than the cost of a prepackaged machine. PC manufacturers, of course, buy their parts in large quantities at wholesale prices.

In other words, it makes no economic sense to completely rebuild an older system with new parts. (It may make sense to you for other reasons, but not when you apply a cold eye to the bottom line.)

Before you go shopping for upgrade components, sit down with a computer spreadsheet (or a pad and pen, which works pretty well, too) and lay out your plans and the cost of each element of the project.

The basic question is this: Does it make sense to upgrade an older machine, or is it time to get a new computer?

Let's start by looking at the cost of the individual components of a very fast basic PC, with prices as they were in mid-2000:

64 MB RAM	$75
Pentium III 600-MHz CPU	$300
AGP video card	$100
Sound card	$70
Windows keyboard	$20
1.44-MB 3.5-inch floppy drive	$20
12-GB IDE hard drive	$110
52X CD-ROM	$45
Internal Zip drive	$100
Scrolling wheel mouse	$20
Motherboard with built-in USB support, AGP slot	$150
Case and power supply	$60
Total:	$1,070

As you can see, this hypothetical bill lands smack in the middle of the magic range I identified earlier for a new machine.

One more thing, most computer manufacturers include the operating system and a suite of applications in their price. If you were building a new machine from scratch, you'd also have to obtain a copy of Windows plus applications software, which can cost several hundred dollars more.

As I've noted, the sum of the parts of a completely rebuilt PC is going to be equal to or greater than the cost of a whole new machine. There's not much sense in spending $1,200 to upgrade a *used* older machine when a *new* and improved model sells for the same price.

Instead, the savvy computer owner picks and chooses the best projects for upgrading. A project costing a few hundred dollars generally makes eminent sense for most older machines. A few judiciously chosen projects can extend the life of a computer by several years.

And while we're on the subject of parts and prices, let's consider a few extras not usually included in an off-the-shelf PC:

CD-recorder or rewritable	$150–$350
DVD-ROM player	$100–$200
Tape backup system	$600
Desktop scanner	$100–$300
Slide scanner	$300–$1,000

Here are some good reasons to upgrade an older PC in good working order:

1. To **boost storage space** by replacing an older, slower hard drive with a faster, larger model, or adding a second, third, or fourth drive.

2. To **improve the speed** of the machine by adding memory.

3. To **perform a brain transplant** by replacing an older microprocessor with a faster and more advanced CPU.

4. To **add or upgrade a CD-ROM** to a faster or more capable model.

5. To **install advanced multimedia features**, such as a current sound card, a DVD-ROM for movies, a screen camera, or a video input device.

6. To **improve input and output capabilities** by adding technologies for faster or easier interconnection of internal and external devices including scanners, digital camcorders, and specialized storage devices. Upgrades include USB, SCSI, FireWire, ATA/66, or additional serial and parallel ports.

7. To **make use of a USB port** to expand the capabilities of a PC.

8. In unusual circumstances, to **replace an outdated motherboard** with a model that includes more current features and will work with most or all of your existing components.

These eight reasons are based on solid technical and economic common sense. There is one more reason:

9. You may want to upgrade your older PC because you are the sort of person who insists on having **full control over the systems in your home or office** and who enjoys the process even if the bottom line doesn't always add up to logical dollars and sense.

PC Life Cycles

By most measures, a PC you might buy or build today has a useful life of two to four years. That doesn't mean your PC will stop functioning a few years after it is first plugged in. What it does mean is that the rapid pace of change in the PC market makes today's wonder hardware seem like antiques after just a few years.

Your PC will still work with the software and peripherals you already have in place, but the next generation of applications and devices will be beyond its reach.

When I appraise the march of PC progress, I think of three classes of change:

■ **Compatible progress.** Improvements to computer technology that can be applied to systems using existing ports, slots, and connectors.

■ **Incompatible progress.** Improvements that require types of microprocessors, motherboards, interfaces, or connectors that don't exist on older systems and cannot be added.

■ **Progress by modification.** Improvements that require modifications to older systems before they can be used.

Examples of **compatible progress** are fast and large hard drives that can be added to a system or installed as replacements for an older, slower drive. You can also upgrade your PC with a new or improved Zip drive, CD-ROM, or DVD-ROM. And you can add memory to an older system, one of the best and easiest upgrade projects.

An example of **incompatible progress** is AGP video. This class of graphics card communicates directly with the microprocessor without having to traverse the crowded system bus of the computer. AGP graphics cards require a specific type of connector, mounted in an unusual position in the center of the motherboard. Most current motherboards offer an AGP slot. There is no way to use an AGP video adapter in a PCI slot, and there is no way to modify an older motherboard to offer an AGP slot.

An example of **progress by modification** is the addition of one or more USB ports, a speedy and easy-to-use version of the original serial port. USB allows users to plug-and-play a wide variety of devices in an expanding chain, without the need to deal with IRQ and memory settings. Current motherboards generally ship with a pair of USB ports already installed; although motherboards from systems produced before mid-1998 probably lack the ports, most older motherboards can accept a plug-in PCI bus adapter that adds a pair of USB ports.

The Building Blocks of a Modern PC

The modern PC is made up of five major building blocks, each with subsystems that can be replaced or upgraded.

- **Case and power supply.** The case holds all of the pieces in their proper position and contains the power supply that runs all of the internal components. A case can be upgraded to a larger or more capacious model. The power supply can be improved to provide more power for internal devices.

- **Motherboard, microprocessor, memory, and components.** The motherboard is the superhighway that connects all of the internal parts. Mounted on the board are the microprocessor and the RAM (random access memory). The motherboard, microprocessor, and RAM can each be upgraded, but they must maintain compatibility with each other; for example, an older motherboard is not likely to work with current CPUs or RAM designs.

- **Storage.** Applications and data are held in more-or-less permanent storage on one or more of the drive subsystems of a PC. These include hard drives, floppy disk drives, CD-ROMs, DVD-ROMs, and removable storage devices such as Zip drives and tape backups. On most PCs, any of these devices can be upgraded to current versions.

- **Input/output devices.** Your PC communicates with you and the outside world through plug-in devices including keyboards, mice, modems, scanners, digital cameras, network interface cards, and ports (serial, USB, parallel, SCSI, and other protocols). Most computers can work directly or, with adaptation, with updated versions of these devices.

- **Graphics and multimedia.** Video adapters and sound cards that plug into the system bus provide your computer's face and voice. In most systems, these devices can be updated to current versions. External multimedia components, including amplified speakers, MIDI devices, and video capture devices, can be added.

In This Book

In this book we'll explore ten hands-on upgrading projects.

Storage
- Installing a larger and faster **hard drive** as a replacement for an existing drive or as an additional drive.

- Adding a **CD-ROM** or **DVD-ROM** or replacing an older CD-ROM with a more modern model.

- Installing a **CD-R** or **CD-RW** to make your own disks.

Backup

- Installing a **Zip drive** for backup and transport of large files.

- Adding an external **Superdisk** drive as an alternate storage device.

- Configuring a **tape backup** system.

Memory

- Adding **RAM** to a system to improve speed and multitasking.

I/O (Input/Output)

- Updating a PC to add **USB** ports.

- Adding **FireWire** ports.

- Installing and using a **SCSI** adapter.

- Adding extra or upgraded **parallel** or **serial ports**.

- Installing and configuring a **network interface card**.

Sight and Sound

- Installing a state-of-the-art **graphics card**.

- Adding a current **sound card**.

Brain Surgery

- Give your PC a brain transplant by installing a faster or more modern **microprocessor** or a specialized processor upgrade.

- Update your machine's basic training with a **BIOS** upgrade.

Eyes and Ears

- Configuring and using external multimedia devices including a **digital camera**, **film scanner**, and **QuickLink**.

USB Devices

- Extending a PC with **USB devices** including hub, keyboard, mouse, camera, and modem.

A Place to Hold Your Stuff

- Perform radical surgery by replacing your machine's original **motherboard** with a more current model.

- Update your PC's **case**.

- Improve system cooling with **fans**.

Minimum Requirements

All of the projects in this book should work with PCs based on Intel **Pentium II** and **Pentium III** microprocessors and compatible motherboards, with systems based on close-cousin Intel **Celeron** chips and with compatible competitors from AMD including systems that use **Athlon, K6-III,** or **K6-2** CPUs. Carefully selected upgrade projects for a Pentium II, Pentium III, or an equivalent Celeron or AMD system make good sense.

Many of the projects will also work with computers that are a few steps behind, including those based on the original Intel **Pentium** chip and the close-equivalent **AMD K-5** CPU. These machines are capable of running most contemporary software, and most can accept, or be adapted to accept, most current hardware devices.

Older machines based on Intel **486** microprocessors don't warrant a great deal of upgrade effort or expense, although if you have one of these systems and it is performing well with basic computing tasks such as word processing or telecommunications, it may make sense to install more memory, a larger hard drive, or improved input and output ports.

Be even more careful with upgrade projects for older machines. In general, projects such as adding more RAM or a larger hard drive make sense; you can also install a USB port and build up a collection of external devices that could one day be transferred to a faster, more current machine. In my opinion, it does not make sense to install a new motherboard in an older machine because in most cases you will not be able to reuse your existing microprocessor, memory, and some or all of the adapter cards.

Summary

We've taken a look at some of the economics of PC components. In the next chapter, I present a news-you-can-use course in PC technology to help you decide on appropriate upgrade projects.

about the author

Corey Sandler was present at the birth of the PC, and has been writing about computers ever since. The first Executive Editor of *PC Magazine*, he went on to edit several national magazines including *Digital News*.

Sandler has written more than 100 books on computer hardware and software subjects, as well as books on travel and consumer finance. He built from scratch the four most current computers in his office.

You can write to the author by e-mail, at:

csandler@econoguide.com

A web site of his books and links to other useful pages is available at:

www.econoguide.com

To send postal mail, write to the author at:

Corey Sandler
Word Association/Econoguide
P.O. Box 2779
Nantucket, MA 02584

Please enclose a stamped, self-addressed envelope if you'd like a reply.

CHAPTER 1

A Short Course in Computer Components

Before we begin the process of upgrading a machine to current specifications, let's spend a bit of time exploring the elements of the computer.

We're not going to get down to the bits and bytes, sectors and platters, nands and nops of computer hardware and microprocessors. Instead, let's talk about *news you can use*. The goal in this chapter is to understand the components of a current PC so that we can take advantage of its modular design and install upgrades that improve the capabilities and speed of the machine.

I'll explain more about some of the details of these components a bit further on in this book as we come to upgrade projects.

We have already seen how the modern PC is made up of five major building blocks, each with subsystems that can be replaced or upgraded:

- Case and power supply

- Motherboard, microprocessor, memory, and components

- Storage

- Input/output devices

- Graphics and multimedia

Let's go through each of the blocks in detail.

Case and Power Supply

The computer's *case* serves two essential purposes: to hold the pieces of the machine in a secure, electrically interconnected chassis, and keep RF (radio frequency) radiation within its covers. It also holds the *power supply* to convert wall current to DC voltage for the PC's internal devices.

Modern cases have larger power supplies, more fans for cooling, and plenty of internal space to hold a wide variety of devices including hard drives, CD-ROMs, removable media storage such as Zip drives, and much more. Today's cases are also designed with rear openings that mate with the expanded input and output ports of current motherboards that include USB ports, AGP video, and other features added in recent years.

New cases also provide easier access to the interior.

I'll discuss cases in more detail in Chapter 12.

Motherboard, Microprocessor, Memory, and Components

The largest and most complex piece of electronics in the PC is the *motherboard*, sometimes called the *mainboard*.

The motherboard is the world headquarters of your PC; sooner or later, everything that happens in the computer traverses its superhighways and side streets, passing through the microprocessor (also called the *CPU* or *central processing unit*) and taking up temporary residence in the system RAM.

The superhighway is the *bus*, a stretch of wires (called *traces*) within the motherboard that carries data and instructions to and from the microprocessor, memory, devices attached to the bus, and to and from input/output ports. In functional terms, the traces are extensions of the address lines within the microprocessor.

Over the course of the history of the PC, there have been half a dozen bus designs, each improving on the previous in terms of speed and ability to work with more than one device at a time.

Devices that commonly plug into a computer's bus include video, sound, network, and internal modem cards.

Today's motherboards almost all use a PCI bus; some systems feature a secondary set of sockets that use the older, slower ISA bus. For the purposes of this book, these are the only buses we will discuss; older designs, including EISA, MCA, and VL, are no longer supported by manufacturers and upgrades to systems based around them are not realistic.

A third type of specialized bus on modern motherboards is the AGP (accelerated graphics port), which is used only for a particular class of video cards. A single AGP socket is offered in addition to the PCI bus for other devices.

There is no way to upgrade or change the bus structure of a motherboard. Once an ISA, always an ISA. However, you can add specialized buses that extend the capabilities of the system; examples of these add-ons include USB (universal serial bus), FireWire, and SCSI.

That's not to say that you can't perform major surgery on your PC to remove an older motherboard and replace it with a newer design. In doing so, you'll have to match the motherboard with a case, power supply, CPU, memory, adapter cards, and disk drives. If you're changing from an older design, you may find that few, if any, of your older devices can be reused after the surgery.

I'll discuss motherboards in more detail in Chapter 12.

The *microprocessor* is the computer's brain, issuing instructions and moving data from place to place within the machine and to devices. It plugs into a special socket on the motherboard and is surrounded by a set of support chips that helps manage the bus and peripherals and by the BIOS chip, which carries the basic instructions the computer needs to "boot up" when it is first turned on.

Different classes of microprocessor require different types and sizes of sockets and support chips. It is generally easy to upgrade *within* a chip family, for example, from a Pentium II 300-MHz to a Pentium II 400-MHz microprocessor, or within most of the CPUs (but not all) in the Pentium III family. Check with the manufacturer of your motherboard or the PC system to determine the type of socket on the motherboard and the capabilities of the surrounding chipset.

It is possible to make some adaptations; for example, an inexpensive circuit board plugs into a slot 1 socket (intended for Pentium II and most

Pentium III microprocessors) to allow you to use a less-expensive Celeron processor. Computer supply dealers also sell adapter cards that convert a Pentium PGA slot (intended for high-end Pentium III microprocessors) to a slot 1 socket.

A handful of motherboards include two microprocessor sockets, allowing users to choose between a Celeron or Pentium II or III CPU.

I'll discuss microprocessors in more detail in Chapter 9.

Another essential element of the motherboard is system *memory*, or *RAM*. Memory is the workspace for your computer, the place where data, instructions, and graphics are held while the microprocessor issues instructions for its movement or manipulation.

All current consumer-level PCs use blocks of memory installed on small circuit boards called *SIMMs* (single inline memory modules) or *DIMMs* (dual inline memory modules). These small cards plug into special connectors on the motherboard; a few unusual designs put the connectors on a plug-in board that attaches to the motherboard.

SIMMs have 72 pins, or edge connectors, which mate with receptacles in the connector; faster and larger DIMMs, which place memory on both sides of the module, have 168 pins. Notebooks and laptop computers use smaller but similar SODIMM (small outline DIMM) modules with 144 pins.

Most motherboards offer either SIMM or DIMM connectors; a handful have sockets for either type.

Once you've determined the type of socket on the motherboard, you'll also need to know the specific type of memory used in the system. Until about 1998, modern machines ran their system bus at 66 MHz; more recently, bus speeds have increased to 100 MHz and 133 MHz. Among the fastest current memory types are SDRAM (synchronous dynamic random access memory) in the PC100 and PC133 variants for the higher-speed buses and a specialized type of memory called *Rambus*.

Your best bet is to gather up the instruction manuals and specification sheets for your motherboard or system and then consult with one of the major memory sellers by telephone or over the Internet; many online pages allow you to enter the model name for your PC and find out the recommended memory type.

In general, it's a bad idea to mix different speeds or types or memory in a system. Do so only with the recommendation—and guarantee—of a memory seller.

I'll discuss memory in more detail in Chapter 6.

When you turn off the power, all of the information in standard RAM disappears in a puff of electrons.

PCs use storage devices such as hard disk drives, floppy disk drives, CD-ROMs, removable media devices such as Zip drives, tape backups, and other such devices to hold onto copies of programs and data when the system is not under power.

Most of these devices use a rotating medium with a metallicized surface and one or more heads that write magnetic notations and can later read them back. Tape backup devices make their records on a moving ribbon.

CD-ROMs and their close cousins DVD-ROMs use focused laser beams to read markings on a plastic disk.

How ever the information is recorded, the goal is the same: to provide mass storage; and the concept of mass storage seems to be expanding day by day. The first PCs had no hard drives at all; the operating system, programs, and data were stored on one or two large, slow floppy disk drives, with a total of about half a megabyte of space. Today, the Windows 98 operating system can take up as much as 300 MB of space all by itself; applications such as Microsoft Office can demand more than 100 MB, and data files including web pages, graphics, and sound files can demand tens of megabytes.

The good news has been the plummeting price of storage. In 1982, soon after the arrival of the IBM PC, the cost per megabyte for a hard disk was about $150 to $300. In 2000, high-speed disks cost about a penny or two per megabyte.

These devices are, by definition, permanent storage, but permanence is relative. The smart computer user never has only one copy of important data or programs. Drives are mechanical devices; it's not a question of whether they will eventually fail, but of determining exactly when.

Until fairly recently, the lowly floppy drive was an essential part of all PCs. It was used to load new programs onto the hard drive and to create disks to transfer files from one machine to another. Today, the floppy disk is no longer the primary device for either task.

Today, nearly all new software is loaded from a CD-ROM disc, which can hold as much as 650 MB of information on a nearly indestructible platter. The 1.44-MB capacity of a floppy disk drive is woefully inadequate for the transfer of many of today's bloated data files; the media of choice for physical transfer of files include Zip disks, Superdisks, and CD-Rs.

I'll discuss drives in more detail in Chapter 4.

Input/Output Devices

The very first computers were islands unto themselves. The operators posed a mathematical question by turning dials or setting switches; the computer, which was in some ways closer to a knitting machine than an electronic calculator, clicked and clacked for a while and then registered an answer on another set of dials or switches.

It took many years before computers were able to accept input from devices such as keyboards, mice, sensors, scanners, cameras, and more. And it took just as long before the first printers, modems, and external storage devices could be attached and used.

The first PCs were delivered with two basic input and output channels: serial and parallel.

The simpler of the two channels is parallel, which is an extension of the data bus of the computer. In its original form, the eight 0s or 1s of a computer word moved in parallel alongside each other like cars on an eight-lane highway; when they arrived at their destination a single byte of information could be read across the width of the eight lines.

Parallel signals were only reliable for a relatively short distance before they dropped bits or were out of sync with each other.

From the start, parallel ports on computers were used to connect to printers. In more recent times, advances to the parallel specification have allowed the cables to communicate in both directions, permitting scanners and other external devices to connect in this way.

The other original interface for PCs is the serial port. Think of this as a reliable one-lane road; the information on a modern computer, which travels on 8-, 16-, or 32-bit-wide highways within the computer must merge—in proper order, one bit behind the other—at the exit port. If it sounds like a traffic jam in the making, you're right. The computer uses a device called a *UART* (universal asynchronous receiver transmitter) and a block of special-purpose memory called a *buffer* to store data and then string the bits in single file or to reverse the process for incoming data.

Serial ports are used for keyboards and mice; they are also well suited for use with modems, because bits of information move over telephone wires in the same serial fashion, one behind the other.

In recent years, the serial interface has been turbocharged with the introduction of the high-speed, flexible USB (universal serial bus) protocol and speedy FireWire. The latest motherboards come with one or both in place, but either can be added to most recent systems.

I'll discuss input and output options in more detail in Chapter 7.

Graphics and Multimedia

Video adapters are the artists behind the spectacular displays on computer monitors. Few components of the PC have advanced so dramatically, or so obviously, as have video adapters.

Today's video adapters work from a palette of millions of colors, painting sharp, detailed images and text on monitor screens.

At the same time, sound cards have moved from the primitive squawks and beeps of the first PCs to systems that can emulate all of the sounds of an orchestra or speak to us in humanlike voices.

I'll discuss video and sound cards in more detail in Chapter 8 and multimedia devices such as scanners and digital cameras in Chapter 10.

CHAPTER 2

Getting Ready To Upgrade

This is a how-to book about upgrading your PC, something in which I believe very strongly. But I will be the first to admit that not every PC is worthy of the time, effort, and expense of an upgrade.

As we have seen, although technology continues to advance at a rapid pace, not all improvements can be applied to older machines. And not all of the decisions are based solely on technology; it's just as important to decide whether it is worth several hundred dollars for a new processor or nearly that much for more RAM and a larger hard drive, or whether the best upgrade is the purchase of a new machine.

Begin by taking a cold, hard look at your machine and decide which elements are candidates for upgrade.

Before you proceed, fill out this form for each PC you are considering working on:

SYSTEM INVENTORY

Processor (486, Pentium, Pentium II, Pentium III,
AMD, Cyrix, Other)   _____

Processor speed   _____

Random access memory type (SDRAM, PC-100, etc.)   _____

Random access memory amount   _____

Hard drive (capacity, available space)   _____

CD-ROM (speed, special features)   _____

Other removable drives (Zip, tape, etc.)   _____

Motherboard manufacturer   _____

Bus slots (PCI, ISA, other)   _____

Cards installed in PCI bus (video, modem, sound,
network, other)   _____

Cards installed in ISA bus   _____

Bus slots available for use (PCI)   _____

Bus slots available for use (ISA)   _____

Special slots (AGP video, modem riser)   _____

Serial ports   _____

Parallel port   _____

SCSI port   _____

USB port   _____

Other port   _____

Notes on special features   _____

Some users may know the answers to all of these questions off the top of
their heads. For the rest of us, there are several ways to fill out the inventory form:

1. Consult the instruction manual that came with your machine. If you
    ordered a machine from a mail order company, you may also have a
    detailed "build" or shipping document that lists all of the components.

Be sure to add to the inventory any memory or other components installed after you receive the machine.

2. Use a system information program that reports on components of a machine running under Windows 95 or 98. These utilities are generally accurate, although some may give false or incomplete reports on devices that are not plug-and-play compliant and on some processors from sources other than Intel. Examine the report carefully and check it against your own knowledge of the machine and any system specifications you have from the manufacturer.

Examples of system information reports, in this case from an element of Norton Systemworks from Symantec, are shown in Figures 2.1 and 2.2.

3. Look under the covers. Place the unit on a sturdy work surface with adequate lighting. Unplug the system from the power source and disconnect all cables (label the cables and the connectors on the PC to make reinstallation easy). Remove the screws or other fasteners that hold the cover in place. (Consult the instruction manual for specifics about your particular machine.) Look into the unit to examine the components. You may need to remove some cards from the bus to inspect them or to clear the way to look closely at the motherboard.

Figure 2.1

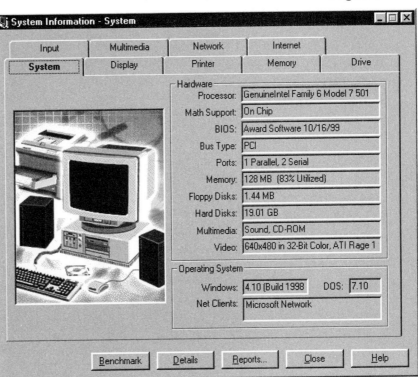

A system information report.

The Right Tools for the Job

There is nothing like having the right tool for the job. Yes, you can bend a paper clip to serve as a screw holder or file down the blade of a screwdriver to make it fit through a hole it was never intended to negotiate. You can also haul manure in the back seat of a Porsche or go skiing in sandals.

Before you attempt to repair or upgrade your PC system, spend the time to equip yourself to do the job right. The work will be much easier, the results more satisfying, and you'll be able to convince just about anyone that you really know what you're doing. All this for less than $50.

Figure 2.2

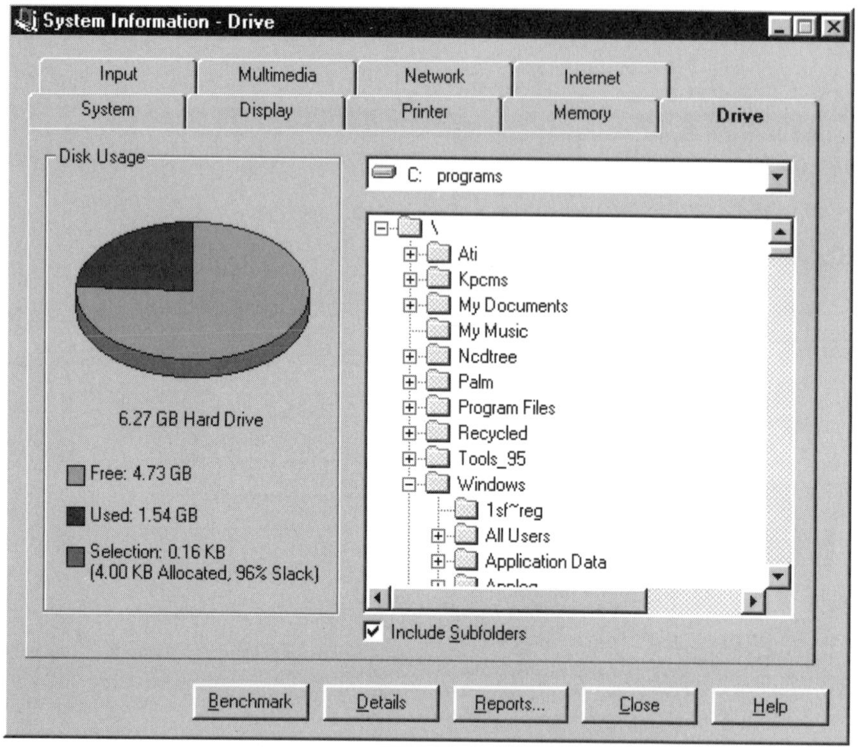

Exploring the system's hard drives.

Start by preparing an appropriate workspace. Pick a solid table or work surface with sufficient room for your PC, your tools, and a notepad. I prefer a table with a white top so that I can easily find dropped screws and other parts.

Make certain you have sufficient lighting. One good setup is a strong overhead lamp and a small, movable task light that can be adjusted as work continues. When I'm working deep inside a PC case I sometimes use a small high-intensity flashlight.

A typical PC uses eight or ten different types, lengths, and diameters of screws. Place alongside your PC a storage container with multiple compartments—a fishing tackle or sewing box, for example, or an empty egg carton; I use plastic film canisters. Label each holder with masking tape and a marker as you fill them with screws.

And keep that roll of masking tape and marker nearby to apply labels to any connector or cable you disconnect.

Have a notebook and pen nearby and make notes as you perform each step. If you remove six screws from the rear of the case, indicate that in your journal and place those screws in a container or compartment that identifies their source.

Finally, make some provision for discharging static electricity from your body. The most professional solution is to use an antistatic strap that runs from a cuff on your wrist to an electrical ground. You can also obtain an antistatic pad that sits on your desktop; a wire from the pad runs to ground. The least impressive way to accomplish the same effect is to make a point of touching electrical ground once you are seated at the work area.

What is a proper electrical ground? In most homes and businesses with electrical systems that are up to code, the center screw on an electrical outlet is connected to ground; you can attach an antistatic strap or pad to the screw or touch the screw with your finger to discharge static electricity.

Another good conduit to electrical ground is a metallic cold water pipe; plastic pipes won't do the trick, and hot water and heating pipes may have their path to ground by a furnace. A less perfect way to discharge static electricity is to touch ground one of the major components of the computer, such as the power supply, before handling electronic parts.

If your home or office is very prone to static buildup, consider making a long-term change in the atmosphere. You can purchase antistatic sprays to apply to carpeting; when you decorate an office area, you can purchase carpeting with a built-in antistatic treatment. You can also buy a special doormat that connects by wire to electrical ground.

A Basic Computer Kit

The basic tool kit for computer upgrade includes a small-diameter Phillips head screwdriver, a small-diameter flat head screwdriver, and small tweezers.

Some computer and peripheral makers, including Compaq at one point in its history, used nonstandard Torx screws to discourage ordinary users from opening the box; the proper way to open a Torx screw is to use a Torx screwdriver with its unusual star-shaped head. A flat-blade screwdriver is occasionally needed on some peripherals.

I also recommend you add to your kit a three-claw parts holder, a valuable tool to hold screws and jumpers in places too small for your fingers.

If you're going to be working on the motherboard, a chip extractor is a specialized form of tweezers with hooked prongs, which fit underneath the sides or edges of a chip in a socket to allow you to safely and easily remove the chip. A chip inserter is a tool that holds an electronic circuit squarely for precise placement in a socket.

For convenience, a ratchet bit handle and a set of changeable bits makes it easier to work on screws on the outside of the case and in some places where a screwdriver may not fit or would be difficult to turn.

You can assemble your own group of tools or purchase a ready-made kit from a computer supply house. Expect to pay between $25 and $100 for a package.

For upgrades, and even for most repairs, these are the things you don't need: a sophisticated voltage meter or other electronic testing device, a soldering iron, or a technician's cable breakout box. Modern equipment has become so modular and inexpensive that it almost always is easier and more efficient to replace a failed component than to attempt to fix it.

Don't even think about taking apart a hard drive or a monitor; these are projects that should only be tackled by an expert, if at all.

A burned-out power supply or a failed internal or external modem are examples of easily swapped components.

Making repairs to a malfunctioning PC is beyond the scope of this book; you may want to consult other books that cover this tricky subject in more detail.

Figure 2.3

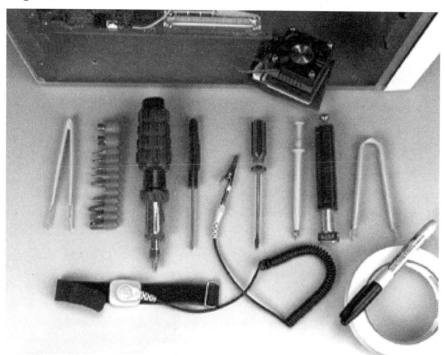

My basic computer tool kit.

My basic tool kit for computer upgrades is shown in Figure 2.3. From left to right is a tweezer; a set of changeable bits; a reversible ratchet bit handle; a small Phillips head screwdriver; a flat head screwdriver; a three-claw parts holder to carry screws to their inaccessible destination or to pick up a dropped screw inside the case; a chip inserter; and a chip extractor tweezer.

Below the tools is an antistatic wrist strap, a roll of masking tape, and a marking pen to label connectors and cables as you work within the PC.

Serious upgraders will also want to have a supply of extra power supply adapters, extensions, taps, and Ys to connect various internal devices to the PC's power supply. A selection from my workbench, along with a spare power supply, is shown in Figure 2.4.

Adapters are used to convert from one type of connector to another, for example, from a power connector intended for a 5¼-inch device to work with one or two 3½-inch devices. A converter that splits one cable to power two devices is called a *Y-adapter*.

Extensions are used to bring power to areas of the case or motherboard that are out of reach of standard power sources; these cables are available in male-to-male, female-to-female, and male-to-female versions.

Taps extend a standard power cable and also branch off with a small connector for low-draw devices such as internal fans.

You can purchase all of these devices from computer supply stores, and you should hold on to extra cables and adapters that come with many devices; they may not be necessary for today's project but may save the day on a future upgrade.

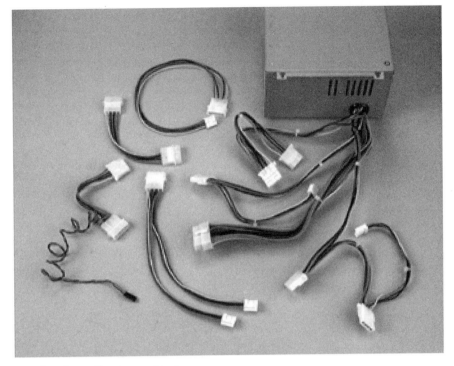

A selection of power adapters.

Another important element of your toolkit should be cable converters, used to mate different types of cables when dealing with unworkable sexual conflicts. Before you get all hot and bothered, that last problem occurs when you find the same gender on a connector and cable or two cables that must be linked.

Figure 2.5 shows a selection of converters from my supply drawer. At top, from left to right, are a 9-pin DB9 serial-to-PS/2 mouse or keyboard connector; a DB9 gender changer female-to-female (male-to-male changers are also available); and a keyboard converter. That last device converts from an old-style 5-pin DIN used on AT systems to the 6-pin mini DIN used with current PS/2 mice or keyboards. In the middle are three converters for data cables. From left to right are a SCSI 1-to-SCSI 3 converter, a

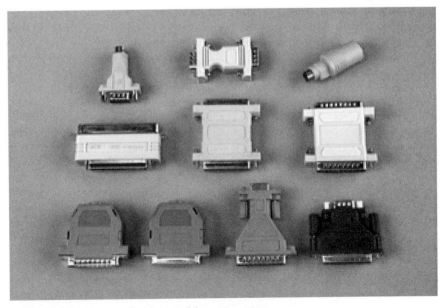

Gender benders and other cable converters.

DB25 female-to-female gender changer, and a DB25 male-to-male gender changer. At the bottom, from left to right, are a pair of loopback plugs used in testing and diagnostics of a serial or parallel port using DB25 connectors, a converter from DB25 male to DB9 male, and a converter from DB25 female to DB9 female.

One of the most important tools in the kit is a safety device: an antistatic wrist strap, like the one shown in Figure 2.6.

Figure 2.6

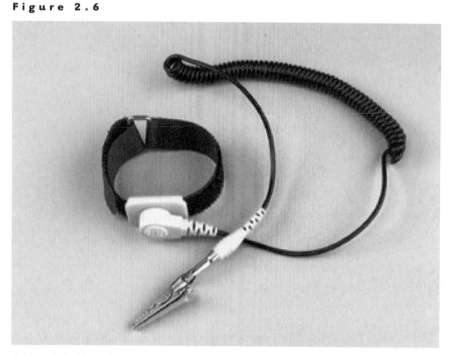

An antistatic wrist strap.

Anyone who has scuffed heels across a carpeted floor and then touched another person knows the power of static electricity. Consider, then, the effects of a jolt of static voltage on a delicate piece of electronics such as a memory chip or a microprocessor.

Before you undertake any upgrade project, take the time to find a way to ground yourself before you touch electronic parts.

This particular strap ends with an alligator clip that can attach to an electrical ground; the wire can detach from the wrist strap for convenience.

Other types of antistatic devices include touchpads that sit on the desktop, with a wire that leads to ground.

In a pinch you can make your own antistatic device by running a copper wire from the center screw of a grounded electrical outlet or from a grounded cold water pipe to a bare wire on your desktop.

CHAPTER 3

A Humble Beginning: Our Demonstration Machine

As I've noted, the projects in this book can be applied to most machines using the Pentium, Pentium II, and Pentium III microprocessors and to equivalent machines including those using Intel Celeron, AMD, and Cyrix microprocessors. Some of the projects, including memory and storage upgrades, can also be performed on systems based on Intel 486 microprocessors, although you should examine very closely the costs and benefits of spending new money on a very old machine.

For the purposes of this book, I have chosen a PC based on a Pentium 133-MHz microprocessor to use as the example for most of the upgrade projects.

Figure 3.1

The demonstration machine before surgery.

Figure 3.1 shows our humble test bed before the start of surgery. This machine was close to the state-of-the-art when I built it in 1996, using a MicroStar motherboard with both PCI and ISA bus slots. This board was on the market during a period of transition from ISA to PCI slots and from 72-pin SIMM to 168-pin DIMM memory sockets.

I retrieved the motherboard manual from its dusty storage place on my bookshelf to read the specifications.

The CPU socket on the board is a combined socket 5 and 7 design, permitting use of Intel Pentium microprocessors from 75 MHz to 200 MHz in speed. It supports as much as 128 MB of memory in three banks: two pairs of 72-pin SIMM sockets and one 168-pin DIMM socket.

The motherboard has three 32-bit PCI bus slots, two 16-bit ISA slots, and one pair of slots that can be used by either a PCI or ISA device.

Onboard peripherals include one floppy port, two IDE ports for hard drives, two serial ports, and one parallel port.

The computer shows its age in the absence of most of the modern amenities: the system has a small and relatively slow hard drive, no backup device, a first-generation slow CD-ROM, a very basic sound card, and an unextraordinary graphics card.

Before surgery, the machine was working reliably. It ran Windows 98 and the full Microsoft Office applications suite, allowing it to fit in with other more modern machines in my lab.

But the demands of the operating system and current applications were sometimes painfully evident. Booting up Windows 98 took several minutes, multitasking slowed down all of the applications noticeably, and demanding graphics programs such as Adobe Photoshop slowed the machine to a crawl.

The front panel of this old PC, shown in Figure 3.2, tells much of the story of what's inside. First, there's a 12X CD-ROM, considered a speedster at

Figure 3.2

the time but a sluggard when compared with today's 52X and faster devices. The display panel boasts a 133-MHz processor within, a far-distant laggard in any race against a current CPU.

A slow processor, insufficient storage, and an outdated CD-ROM.

Behind the blank front plate is a still functional but puny (by today's standards) 540-MB hard drive.

The back panel also shows the limited selection of I/O options. From top to bottom, Figure 3.3 shows an old-style 5-pin AT connector for a keyboard, a full-size DB25 serial port, a shared bracket with a parallel port at left and a small DB9 serial port, a monitor cable connector from a basic SVGA graphics card, a set of audio and joystick inputs and speaker outputs from an unsophisticated sound card, and a simple network interface card output for an Ethernet connection.

As I've noted, the machine works, but there's a lot of potential for upgrade here.

Preparing for Surgery

We're now ready to prepare this machine for our upgrade projects. Let's step back in time for a moment to look at the rear of the machine, with many of its cables plugged in, seen in Figure 3.4.

Be sure you have a sturdy work surface and plenty of light. Before you do anything else, unplug the power cord. On this tower machine, the power supply is at the top of unit.

Stop and examine all of the remaining cables before you disconnect them. Use a notepad to make a rough sketch of what you see.

Place masking tape tags on each of the cables and use a marking pen to label them. Put another tag on the connectors themselves or write directly onto the brackets with a marking pen.

Figure 3.3

Limited input and output options.

On most PCs, especially older ones, you'll need to remove six to eight screws to take the cover off.

On a desktop PC, the cover slides back and up to reveal the motherboard, which lies parallel to your desk surface.

On a tower, you'll sometimes have access to both sides of the case—the top and bottom of the motherboard, which lies perpendicular to the floor. For every upgrade task in this book, with the exception of replacement of the motherboard itself, you will not need access to the bottom of the motherboard.

One way to know which side to take off for access to the motherboard is to locate ports that are attached to the motherboard rather than on a bracket that plugs into the bus; on this older system, the only such connection is the keyboard port, indicated on the left in Figure 3.4. This indicates that the side to remove would be to the right.

All that said, on this older case, the entire cover slides off.

Figure 3.4

Preparation for surgery.

Study the screws on the back or side of the case before you remove them; some computer manuals come with diagrams to indicate which of them need to be removed.

For most upgrade projects, you should not remove the set of screws around the power supply fan; they are usually smaller than the screws that hold the case cover in place. The only time you may need to remove these screws, shown in Figure 3.5, is if you are replacing the power supply itself.

As you remove the screws, place them in a marked envelope, box, or container like the plastic film canisters shown in Figure 3.6. Trust me: you'll be thankful you took the extra effort when it comes time to reassemble the system later.

Remove the cover to expose the innards of the case. On this model of tower case, lift the cover up and away, as shown in Figure 3.7. Consult your system's manual for any advice specific to your particular case.

Figure 3.5

Power supply screws.

Move slowly and carefully; do not force the cover and be careful not to pull on any internal cables or devices. When in doubt, stop and examine the interior with a flashlight or desk lamp.

Figure 3.6

Some more current cases require removal of just two screws to slide out one of the side panels. Another group of cases dispenses with screws altogether; sliding side panels snap into place in plastic channels.

The machine with its cover off is shown in Figure 3.8. We've moved away the monitor, the keyboard, and power center to open up a comfortable workspace.

This full-size tower offers a great deal of interior space that is nicely compartmentalized.

Removing the proper case screws.

F i g u r e   3 . 7

Lift the cover up and away.

The power supply sits on a shelf at the back of the box. At the top of the case is a cage that holds three 5¹/₄-inch devices with access to the front of the PC; another cage hangs below and can hold four 3¹/₂-inch devices with two openings to the front of the case. With an adapter kit, a 3¹/₂-inch device can be mounted in the 5¹/₄-inch cage.

When I built this machine, I installed a CD-ROM drive in the upper bay and floppy and hard drives in the lower bay.

Use a vacuum to clear places where air enters and exits the PC, as shown in Figure 3.9. You'll be surprised (or appalled) at how much gunk will build up over the years. Sometimes it can be enough to block airflow and endanger your system by allowing heat to build up. The faster (and therefore hotter) the CPU you use, the more important it becomes to practice good PC hygiene so that the fans can do their work.

F i g u r e   3 . 8

The demonstration machine is exposed.

Start by applying the vacuum hose to the intake of the power supply fan. Some PC designs, especially more modern ones, have several inflow and out-flow louvers to support multiple fans.

Then move to the interior of the PC, using a brush head or other soft attachment on the hose, as shown in Figure 3.10. If the vacuum has a speed adjustment or airflow setting, use low power. Be careful not to scratch the surface of the motherboard or any adapter cards and don't dislodge cables or wires.

The goal is not to make your PC operating room clean but to remove any dust that will endanger airflow or that could come between a device and its place of attachment, making for a bad electrical connection.

Some PC users prefer to use a can of compressed air to blow away dust and contaminants from within the machine. I'm not a big fan of this technique, because it shoots the dust back into the air where it will fall onto other pieces of equipment in your office. You can use compressed air to scoot away the last remaining pieces of dust in a system after the vacuum has done the heavy cleaning.

Figure 3.9

Vacuuming the air vents.

Before you remove any parts, take a moment to familiarize yourself with the computer's innards. Make notes and rough sketches on a notepad to help with your planning and as an aid for reassembly.

The largest module of the PC is the power supply, shown in Figure 3.11. This component converts incoming wall current into a series of connectors carrying plus and minus 5 and 12 volts for use by various pieces of equipment within the case.

You can spot the power supply in several ways. First of all, you can locate it by examining the rear panel for power plugs and its exhaust fan. You can also

Figure 3.10

Cleaning the inside of the machine.

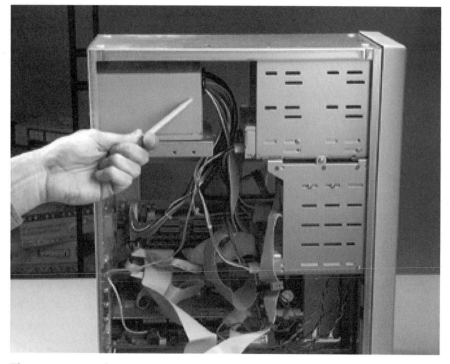

The power supply.

spot the power supply by following the large red, black, yellow, and white wires from the motherboard.

Because the power supply generates heat, PC designers like to place it at the top of a tower case or at the rear of a desktop unit; either location makes it easy to exhaust heat without drawing it over other components of the system. This is one reason it is generally not a good idea to operate a desktop PC in an upright position or a tower case on its side.

The largest block of cables from the power supply connects to the motherboard, as seen in Figure 3.12. Older motherboards using the AT design use two connectors marked P8 and P9; highly integrated ATX motherboards use a single, larger connector to power the system.

The power supply's connection to the motherboard.

By the way, note the precut openings on the back wall of the case; on this model, you can use a heavy screwdriver or punch to break away the metal still in place to install additional connectors to support input and output from the AT motherboard. On current ATX designs, most of the connectors are mounted on the motherboard itself and fit into standardized openings.

Other, smaller electrical cables extend from the power supply to devices. The upper connector shown in Figure 3.13 supplies the CD-ROM drive and the lower powers an internal hard drive.

Data cables move information to and from storage devices. In Figure 3.14, I'm holding the connector to the floppy disk drive; the pointer shows the data cable to an internal hard disk drive.

In this picture you can also see how the lower drive cage slides onto an attaching flange and is held in place by screws. We'll explore drive cages in more detail in Chapter 4, with the hard drive upgrade project.

On our demonstration system, the data cables connect to the hard disk and floppy disk controllers on the motherboard, as seen in Figure 3.15. Some older PCs may have controllers on adapter cards. If you upgrade your PC to add SCSI or advanced ATA/66 hard drive controllers, for example, the drives will also connect to adapter cards instead of directly to the motherboard.

Figure 3.13

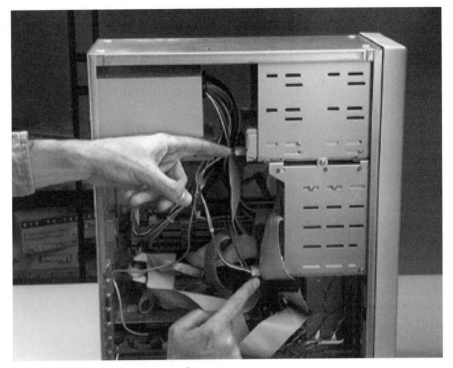

A branch off the power supply.

In Figure 3.15, the cable on the left connects to the floppy drive; to the right, a data cable attaches to the primary IDE connectors; a secondary IDE connector lies open beneath.

The microprocessor was installed in a socket directly on the motherboard from the early days of the PC through the Pentium, as seen in Figure 3.16. With the arrival of the Pentium II, the microprocessor moved to a vertical chip carrier that installed in a slot on the motherboard, a design that is also used for most Pentium III and AMD Athlon CPUs. The

Figure 3.14

Data cables attach to drives.

Figure 3.15

The other end of the data connection is on the motherboard on this system.

most advanced Pentium III and Celeron microprocessors are also available in a version that mounts horizontally on the motherboard.

Figure 3.16 shows the Pentium 133-MHz chip hidden beneath a fan. The large Intel chip to the left of the CPU is part of the system chipset, which performs some of the management of the bus and devices of the PC. It is the chipset that gives a machine its basic personality; in this case, we have a motherboard with PCI and ISA buses. Other chipsets may add features such as AGP graphics pathways, Ultra DMA/66 hard drive controllers, and more. In general, the chipsets are soldered in place on the motherboard and not repairable or upgradeable.

A close-up of the Intel Pentium chip on our demonstration machine, seen in Figure 3.17, shows it locked into place in its socket, beneath a fan.

All Pentium-class microprocessors and many of the faster 486 CPUs require cooling systems to draw away the heat generated by the high-frequency cycles of the chip. In this case, the Pentium 133 is cooled by a small fan that sits atop the chip and is attached by clips at the top and bottom. The fan needs to be connected to one of the branches of the power supply. On some motherboards, there's a small power header near the microprocessor socket for the use of cooling fans.

Figure 3.16

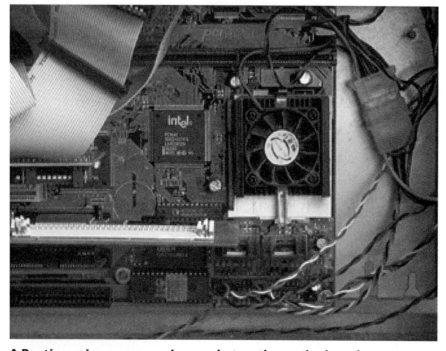

A Pentium microprocessor in a socket on the motherboard.

Other important connection points on the motherboard are the headers, which provide power and data links to front panel displays, the on/off switch, the reset button, turbo switch, and the keylock. On our demonstration machine, the headers are just below the microprocessor, as seen in Figure 3.18.

Don't disconnect these wires without making a careful study and a set of notes about their placement. Consult the manual about the motherboard before making any changes.

On this particular motherboard, to the left of the headers is a socket that holds the BIOS chip, also shown in Figure 3.18. The demonstration PC uses a BIOS developed by AMI; other makers include Phoenix and Award, once separate companies but now merged.

The BIOS manages the start-up sequences for the machine and also works with the chipset to establish the system's personality.

In many cases, the BIOS chip can be replaced or upgraded with software to add current features and deal with compatibility issues with devices and software not envisioned when the chip was first put in place. Consult with the maker of your motherboard or with a BIOS vendor to learn about upgrade options. I'll discuss BIOS upgrades in Chapter 9.

RAM is installed on the motherboard on small carriers that

Figure 3.17

The Pentium is cooled by a clip-on fan.

Figure 3.18

Motherboard connections and the BIOS chip.

Figure 3.19

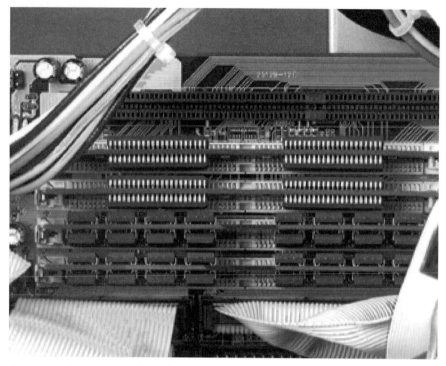

SIMMs on the motherboard.

Figure 3.20

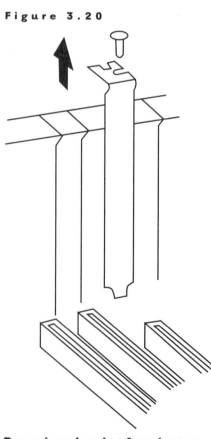

Removing a bracket for adapter card installation.

plug into special memory slots. (The very first PCs worked with individual memory chips that plugged into rows of sockets on the motherboard.)

On this motherboard, which appeared during the transition from SIMMs to faster and higher-capacity DIMMs, there are four 72-pin SIMM slots and a single 168-pin DIMM slot.

At the time I built the machine, DIMMs were more expensive and relatively scarce. As seen in Figure 3.19 before the upgrade, I populated the machine with memory using four SIMMs (of two different but compatible designs). The DIMM socket above the SIMMs stands empty.

If you are working with an older, hybrid motherboard such as this one, check the instruction manual to see whether both types of memory carriers can be used in the same machine. In some designs, if you use the DIMM slot, you cannot use all of the banks of memory ordinarily claimed by SIMMs.

On this particular older motherboard, each bank of two SIMM sockets supports 4, 8, 16, or 32 MB (half the memory goes on each side of the bank). Both SIMM banks must be the same type, of equal size, and of the same density. Both 3.3-V and 5-V SIMMs can be used, but if you use the DIMM slot, only 3.3-V devices can be used. The DIMM slot constitutes a bank to itself.

Many of the features of a current PC are added to the system with adapter cards that plug into the bus. The most common bus design, used in nearly all current motherboards, is called PCI. An older and slower bus design, called ISA, is sometimes present on current motherboards to allow use of older cards.

Adapter cards ease into place in the bus and are held in place by a bracket that attaches to the case. To add a new card, you'll need to remove a dummy bracket, as shown in Figure 3.20. The new card attaches in its place, slipping between the spring-loaded connectors in the bus slot, as shown in Figure 3.21.

We've completed our tour of the demonstration machine that will be used for most of the upgrade projects in this book.

It should be obvious that the more time you spend in preparation, the easier and quicker the upgrade projects will be accomplished. Locate and study the instruction manual for your motherboard and system. If you don't have a copy, contact the manufacturer of the system for assistance. You may find resources on web pages offered by the motherboard maker or the system manufacturer.

Once you have studied the specifications, conduct a survey of the system itself to learn about any modifications or upgrades already in place. You can use system tools within Windows or utilities to determine the type of processor in place and the amount of memory installed.

Figure 3.21

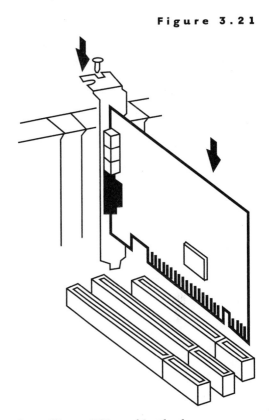

Installing a PCI card in the bus.

CHAPTER 4

Storage Devices

Project 1: Hard Drives, CD-ROMs, DVD-ROMs

Back at the dawn of the PC, everything fit on a floppy disk drive. These were not reliable and relatively capacious 1.44-MB disks in a 3½-inch hard plastic holder like the ones used in most modern PCs, but rather a problematic and very bendable 5¼-inch circle of plastic with a capacity of just 160 KB. If your machine had two disk drives, you hoped to fit the program on one disk and the data on the second disk.

The first hard disk drives arrived with the IBM PC-XT in 1982. Large and slow devices that could hold 10 MB cost about $1,000.

Today, the Windows 98 operating system demands 200 to 300 MB of space all by itself. Common applications need as much as 30 MB. And files, especially those that contain graphics, regularly exceed 1 MB apiece.

Mass Storage Options

Today, the hard drive is an essential element of a desktop PC. The lowly floppy disk drive is still in use as an emergency boot device and for the installation of some smaller software programs. Today, there are now dozens of other storage options, each aimed at a particular use.

A very popular mass storage device is the CD-ROM, an adaptation of the music CD that can hold as much as 650 MB of data; CD-ROMs are now the preferred media for installation of software (CD-ROMs, as the name suggests [CD read-only-memory]). CDs are produced at a factory and cannot be erased or written to by a standard CD-ROM device.

The original CD-ROM drives delivered their data at a poky rate of 150 K per second, which made them all but useless for displaying motion video for multimedia applications. The next generation doubled that speed to 300 K per second and became known as "double-speed," or 2X devices. From there, the race was off and running. Today's speed champs for consumer-level devices deliver data at as much as 8,400 K per second, or about 56X.

The top listed speed for a CD-ROM drive is mostly theoretical; the actual output will depend on where on the disc the data is stored (tracks closer to the center spin faster than those at the outside, for example), how well organized the data on the disc is, and other factors.

If you have a machine with a 12X or slower CD-ROM, an upgrade to a current model should be at the top of your list. If your CD-ROM drive runs at 12X or faster, the decision is less obvious. If you are experiencing problems with the latest and greatest multimedia game or application, a newer CD-ROM may be the cure; otherwise, you may get more bang for the buck by investing in RAM or a faster hard drive.

For about $100 to $200, you can purchase a CD-R (CD recorder) that can use a built-in laser to create your own CDs on special media. CD-Rs can "burn" a 650-MB disc for permanent storage; once created, these discs can be read by any current CD-ROM drive but cannot be altered. (Note that I say CD-Rs can be read by any "current" CD-ROM drive. The first generation of CD-ROM drives, usually single- or double-speed devices, may be unable to read CD-Rs. That's one reason to upgrade an older CD-ROM; the other is to move into the high-speed lane for retrieval of data from all discs.)

The next step up is a CD-RW (CD re-writable) drive. As the name suggests, these devices can write and rewrite to discs, erasing files as needed and recording over them. The mechanism is different from that of a hard drive, but the end result is similar.

CD-RWs require special media for recording, and you may find that the resulting discs can only be read in the machine that created them or similar models. The most current CD-RWs claim to have solved this problem.

Note, too, that CD-Rs and CD-RWs read data much more slowly than current CD-ROM drives. Although you could purchase a 52X CD-ROM for about $50 as this book went to press, the fastest consumer-level CD-Rs could read data no faster than 16X or 20X.

Should you buy a CD-R or a CD-RW? Ask yourself how you will use the device. If you are producing discs to give to someone else to load onto their machine, a CD-R disc (about 50 cents apiece at current prices) will do the job quite well. Compare that cost to CD-RW media (about $2 apiece as this book goes to press). If you expect to reuse a CD-RW disc more than four times, it makes economic sense. In my experience, CD-Rs are a better fit and a better deal for most users.

The solution I use in my office is this: I have 52X CD-ROM drives in most machines for loading programs and reading from data discs, and I have an external CD-R on a networked PC to burn discs for archiving and transport.

And then there are DVD-ROMs, an ultra-high-capacity variation on the CD-ROM theme. These drives pack as much as 4.7 GB of data on one layer, with multiside and multilayer drives already in development. DVD-RAMs, recordable DVD devices, are also available.

DVD-ROMs install in the same way as a CD-ROM, and all of the instructions in this section apply to those devices as well.

In this chapter I'll concentrate on installing internal IDE drives. You can also purchase external drives that connect to the parallel or USB port or to a connector on a SCSI card.

In Chapter 5, I'll discuss removable storage, including Zip drives and tape backup units.

A Short Course in Interfaces

You've got this storage device—a hard drive, a CD-ROM, a DVD-ROM, whatever—and you've got your computer. One is not part of the other, and without the proper connection and an agreed-upon structure for communication, they can't talk to each other.

Together, the connection and communication protocol are called an *interface*. In general, the faster the throughput, in megabytes per second, the better. Some interfaces and associated drives are more expensive to purchase. Over the history of the PC, there have been nearly a dozen interfaces, a steady march that has improved the speed and ease of use.

Today, nearly all current motherboards include a version of the IDE (integrated drive electronics) interface. Until mid-1999, the state of that particular art was a variant called Ultra ATA, also called ATA/33 or DMA/33. Motherboards sold after that moved on to an interface called ATA/66, which doubled the potential throughput to a zippy 66 MB per second.

Most motherboards include two IDE channels, a primary and secondary. Each channel supports two devices, identified to the system as master and slave.

The IDE interface is a relatively simple one; it is an extension of the computer's bus that connects to devices that have an intelligent controller built into the drive. As IDE drives got faster, the interface did not have to change.

You can use any IDE drive with any IDE controller; data will be transferred at the maximum speed of the slower of either end of the connection. In other words, if your older motherboard has an original IDE controller (with a top end of 2 to 3 MB per second) that's the throughput you'll receive, even if it is mated with an ATA/33 drive.

The ATA/66 specification is a bit more demanding. For an ATA/66 drive to deliver data at its top speed you'll need: an ATA/66 drive, a system BIOS that supports ATA/66, and an ATA/66 cable of connecting the drive and the interface.

The ATA/66 cable is a hybrid design that uses a 40-pin connector at the PC end but splits the signal into 80 wires within the cable and at the drive end. On the cable, the blue connector attaches to the interface on the motherboard; the black connector attaches to the master drive on the cable, and the middle connector is used for a slave drive, if used.

You can purchase a simple adapter card to add IDE to an older motherboard; the card is a plug-and-play device. And you can purchase an ATA/66 adapter card as an upgrade; you'll likely need to add special driver software to update your system's BIOS if it was created before support for ATA/66 was included.

In addition to IDE, some systems add support for another interface, SCSI. This interface was once the unchallenged speed champion, although that advantage has faded in the face of ATA/66. Today, SCSI's primary advantage is the ability to daisy-chain one device behind the other from the same interface; SCSI is widely used for external devices including scanners, tape backups, and some older CD-ROM drives. Even that advantage is sure to be eroded in coming years because of the growing—and quickening— USB specification.

I'll discuss adding a SCSI interface in Chapter 7.

Choosing a Hard Drive

Today, a reasonable minimum size for the hard drive in a Windows-based machine is 4 GB. But the prices of drives have come down precipitously at the same time as storage needs have increased dramatically.

I would recommend spending just a few dozen dollars more to install a drive of at least 10 GB in size. If you're going to be working with digital images from a camera or scanner, audio files, or plan to develop your own web page, I'd go at least one notch larger to 20 GB.

In mid-2000, mail order and web page PC outlets sold 4.3-GB hard drives for about $80 to $90, 10-GB drives for about $115 to $125, and 20-GB drives for about $145.

Just as with closet space in your home or apartment, it is truly liberating to have more storage space than you really need; you'll very likely be surprised at how quickly you find ways to fill up the available room.

One state-of-the-art hard disk for consumer systems is the Maxtor DiamondMax Plus 40, shown in Figure 4.1, with its sealed covers removed by the manufacturer; please don't try this at home. This drive squeezes 40 GB of data onto a one-pound drive that fits into a $3^1/_2$-inch bay.

Figure 4.1

Maxtor DiamondMax Plus 40-GB hard drive.

The platters spin at 7,200 RPM, with an average seek speed of less than 9.0 milliseconds. The drive's interface includes a 2-MB cache buffer using high-speed 100-MHz SDRAM memory.

Using an Ultra DMA/66 interface and cable, the drive can transfer information from the interface at up to 66.7 MB per second. The four platters store 10.2 G of data apiece, with one head on each side of the platter.

Making Space for Storage

There are dozens of designs for PC cases. One typical design for a mid-tower offers two to four $5^1/_4$-inch bays that can be accessed from the front of the case, one or two $3^1/_2$-inch bays with front access, and several internal $3^1/_2$-inch bays.

You'll need front access for devices that use removable media, for example, floppy disk drives, Zip drives, CD-ROMs, CD-Rs, CD-RWs, DVD-ROMs, and tape drives.

Most floppy drives and Zip drives will fit in 3½-inch bays; you can add mounting brackets, also called *rails*, to their sides to allow them to fit in a 5¼-inch bay (Figure 4.2).

CD and DVD devices and most tape drives require 5¼-inch bays.

Most current hard disks are designed to fit in a 3½-inch bay; a handful of 5¼-inch drives are also available (Figure 4.3). (Tiny 2-inch drives are intended for use with notebook computers and are not generally cost effective for PCs.)

Figure 4.2

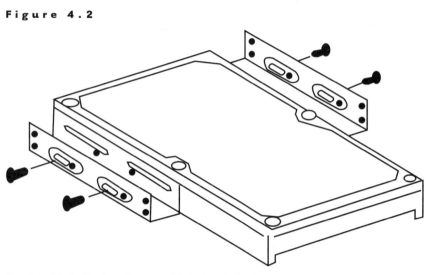

Adding 5¼-inch rails to a 3½-inch device.

Hard drives do not require a bay with access from the outside.

Examine the PC case and determine how the device will be installed. Drives with front access usually are slid into the case from outside, although in some cases you may find it more convenient to come in from the back.

For external access bays, remove the face plate that covers the opening. On some cases a plastic bezel is held in place with clips; metal plates sometimes have to be (carefully) punched out with a screwdriver or twisted out with pliers. Try to pull any metal plate toward you rather than push it into the interior of the case to avoid sending metal slivers into the motherboard.

Figure 4.3

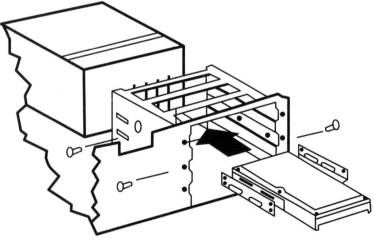

Installing a hard drive in a 5¼-inch bay.

Some internal bays are held in metal cages suspended from the power supply or elsewhere in the case; because they don't require access from the exterior, they can be located anywhere they can be reached by power and data cables. You may find that you need to unhook or

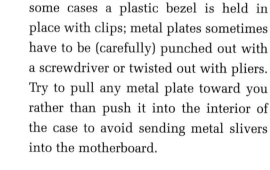

unscrew the cage and remove it from the case so that you have room to install a drive and its cables. Be sure to carefully set aside any screws you remove and mark any disconnected cables and connectors for easy reinstallation later.

If you need to install rails on a 5¹/₄-inch drive so that it will fit in a 3¹/₂-inch device bay, do so when the drive is outside of the case (Figure 4.4). Follow the instructions on the packaging with the rails. Be sure you don't overtighten the screws; doing so could warp or crack the drive's case.

Figure 4.4

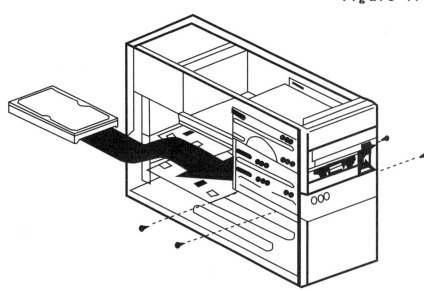

Installing a hard drive in a 3¹/₂-inch bay.

Preparing a Drive Bay for a Hard Drive

To install a floppy or hard drive, CD-ROM or DVD-ROM, or a backup device on our demonstration system, it's necessary to remove one or both of the drive cages. On some case designs, you may also need to remove the cages to replace or upgrade the power supply.

Some PCs do not use drive cages or use cages that are permanently attached to the framework of the case. If you are installing a hard drive into a drive cage that is fixed in place or into a bay that is accessible from the front of the case, skip ahead to the next section.

Study the layout of your PC case and consult the system's instruction manual to familiarize yourself with its mechani-

Figure 4.5

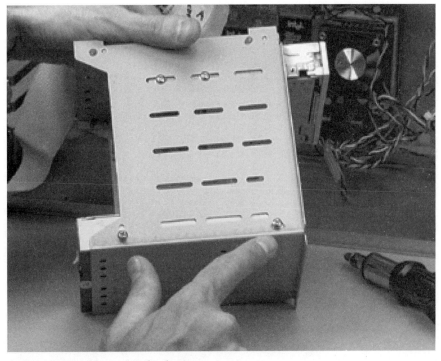

A drive cage for multiple devices.

Figure 4.6

A grounding wire for the drive cage.

cal structure. Make notes and sketches in your notebook to help with reassembly.

In the demonstration PC, shown in Figure 4.5, internal hard drives are mounted in a drive cage that hangs from beneath the power supply; the top two bays match up with external openings in the case for use by devices such as floppy disk drives and Zip drives. The lower two bays can hold 3$\frac{1}{2}$-inch hard drives.

The cage is held in place by two screws at the top and a metal flange that slides into a rail below the power supply.

Drives are held in place by a pair of screws on each side. On most PCs you'll need to remove the cage to gain access to the screws.

In this system, each of the drive bays is connected by a ground wire to the case's frame, shown in Figure 4.6. The frame is in turn electrically connected to the power supply's ground.

Figure 4.7

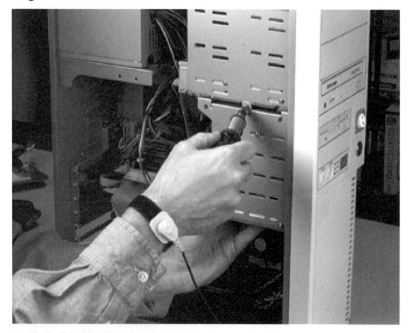

Rails hold the drive cage in place.

The separate ground is a redundant nicety, a belt-and-suspenders sort of design, because the cages are metallic and attached to the metal frame in any case. Nevertheless the extra ground won't hurt and may help reduce or eliminate damage from static electricity and avoid hum on the sound subsystem. Ground wires are usually bright green.

Therefore, before removing this drive bay, we remove the ground wire.

The drive cage is held in place by flanges and is locked with a single screw in this design, shown in Figure 4.7; other cases may have screws on both sides of the drive cage. Be sure to support the cage with your free hand to keep it from falling onto devices below.

Figure 4.8

Remove the drive bay carefully, as shown in Figure 4.8. Take care that you don't clip any wires or damage any devices.

Attach labels to connectors and cables before your remove them. In Figure 4.9, I've noted the purpose of the cable and used an arrow to indicate its orientation as up or down.

Once the cables have been removed, you can move the drive bay out of the way. In Figure 4.9, I am disconnecting the data cable from the hard drive. Note the keyed notches on the top of cable; there is a corresponding slot in the connector on the drive.

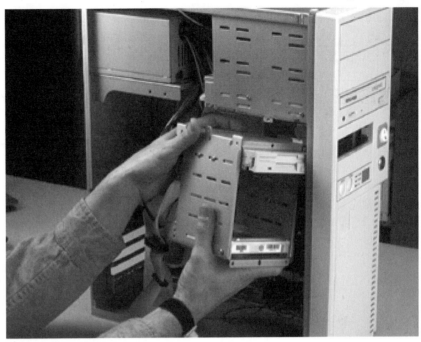

Take care not to damage wires.

Installing the Hard Drive

Ground yourself before you open the sealed plastic bag that holds your new hard drive. On some drive designs, the motor is exposed on the top or the bottom of the drive. Avoid touching the motor or any other exposed mechanical or electronic parts.

Figure 4.9

Check your drive's instruction manual to see if you need to configure drive jumpers. Most hard drives are shipped preset as the master drive on the IDE chain; if the drive is to be the second drive on the cable, you'll need to move a jumper on the back of the drive to identify it as a slave device. An example of a jumper block is shown in Figure 4.10. Place the drive on a white or light-colored surface and use a tweezers to remove jumpers, if necessary, and to install them as instructed by the manual. The light surface will help you find the jumper if you drop it.

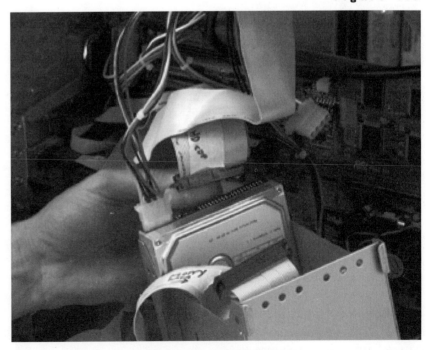

Label connectors and cables for reinstallation.

Figure 4.10

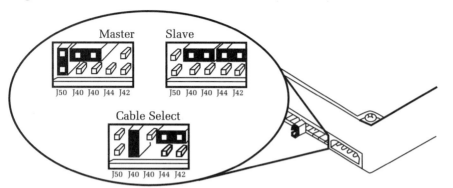

Master/slave jumper block on IDE device.

(There is a relatively rare, special wiring system called Cable Select that allows the system to determine whether a device is a master or slave based on where it is connected on the cable. You'll also need to set a jumper on the hard drive to instruct it to work with the Cable Select wiring.)

Write down the model and serial number from the drive before you install it in the case and make note of any changes you may have made to the jumper block. Noting this information will make it easier to register the drive with the manufacturer and obtain support, if necessary. Store your notes inside the instruction manual for the drive.

Figure 4.11 shows a new drive sliding into place in the drive cage.

Before handling a drive, discharge static electricity from your body by touching an unpainted metal surface on your computer chassis or use an antistatic pad or strap. Don't open the sealed bag for the drive until necessary, and when you do, handle the drive only by the sides. Don't press on the top or bottom of the drive and avoid touching the exposed electronics and motor.

In most systems you'll want to attach power and data cables to a new hard drive before you slide it into a bay, as shown in Figure 4.12. If the drive is going into a drive cage, the cables can be attached after it is screwed into place but before the cage is returned to its position within the case.

An example of data and power connections on an IDE device is shown in Figure 4.13.

Figure 4.11

A new drive slides into place.

For an external bay, bring the cables through the front of the PC and connect them to the drive outside the case.

For an internal bay, make the connections to the drive while you hold it short of the device bay.

Power cables have beveled edges that match the irregular shape of the connector, making it difficult to install them incorrectly. Don't force the cable; be sure it is properly aligned and fully inserted.

Slide the drive into the bay from the back or front as appropriate. Most drives are secured in place in the bay with four screws, two on each side. You may find it helpful to use a screw-holding tool to place screws into their holes in the bay.

Consult the instruction manual for the motherboard or adapter if you have any question about proper installation.

Similarly, the data cable should be keyed with a notch that aligns with a slot in the connector on the drive. On most drives, the notch faces toward the top of the drive; the red or blue stripe on the cable marks pin 1, which almost always is next to the power connector. Check the instruction manual for details about the drive.

Figure 4.12

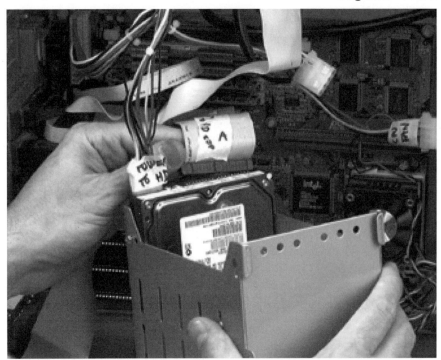

Attach cables to the drive bay before reinstallation.

Figure 4.13

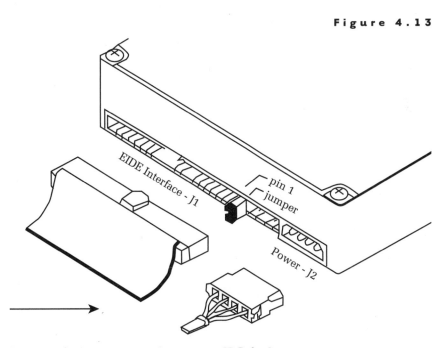

Data and power connections on an IDE device.

You'll need to connect the proper connector on the cable with the master at the end of the cable or with the slave in the middle. An IDE chain will not function if there is a device connected to the slave and not to the master.

IDE devices, including most hard drives, CD-ROMs, and DVD-ROMs connect to an IDE data interface; that port is usually located on the motherboard. On older motherboards or on systems where the hard drive controller has been upgraded, the IDE interface is located on an adapter card in the bus.

The IDE standard has gone through a number of improvements over the years, advancing from the original transfer speed of 2 to 3 MB per second to the latest and greatest version, ATA/66, which can transfer data at 66 MB per second.

IDE, EIDE, and IDE ATA/33 all use the same basic 40-wire cable, with a connector at the end and often a connector in the middle for a second device.

High-speed Ultra ATA/66 devices must use a special cable that matches their needs; using a standard 40-pin IDE cable will result in Ultra ATA/33 performance, a top speed of 33 MB per second.

The ATA/66 cable has three color-coded connectors. The blue connector goes to the system port, the black connector to the master drive, and the gray connector to the slave drive. A diagram of the ATA/66 cable is shown in Figure 4.14.

Figure 4.14

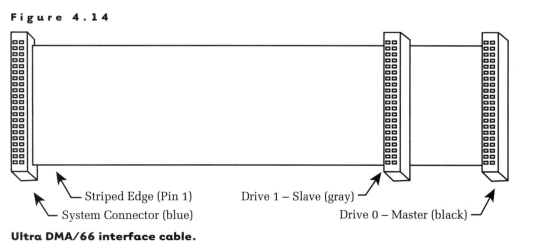

Striped Edge (Pin 1)
System Connector (blue)
Drive 1 – Slave (gray)
Drive 0 – Master (black)

Ultra DMA/66 interface cable.

You may also find some special configurations of Ultra ATA/66 cables that swap the positions of the master and slave devices, putting the master in the middle of the cable.

On both types of IDE cables, the colored edge stripe on the cable matches pin 1 on the IDE connector on the card. If there is only one device on the cable it should be attached to the end connector on the cable and configured as the master device. If you have a second device on the cable, it should attach to the middle connector and be configured as the slave device.

I discussed slave and master settings earlier in this chapter. Remember that an IDE chain will not function if there is a device connected to the slave connector and not to the master, and that a drive identified as a master but attached to the slave connector will not be recognized.

If the data cable is not already attached to an IDE connector on the motherboard or on a hard drive adapter card, install it now. Make sure the cable is properly oriented to the port; the red or blue stripe on the cable marks pin 1, and the connector on the port should be marked for pin 1.

Figure 4.15

If you're using a drive cage, slide the completed package back into place. In Figure 4.15, I have installed power and data cables to the hard drive and the floppy drive into the cage.

Completing the Drive Installation

The next step in the hard drive installation is to help your PC's BIOS work with the capabilities of your new drive.

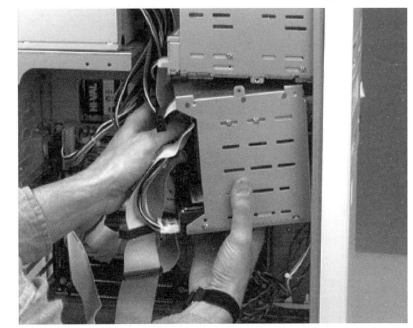

The drive cage reattaches to its rails.

Check the instruction manual that comes with most hard drives and the manual for your PC to see if there are any particular special steps for your drive or computer.

Boot up your computer and go to the BIOS set-up screen. You should see an instruction as the machine boots up, telling you how to display the set-up program; on some systems you'll need to press the Del key, whereas other BIOS systems require other keys such as F2.

Consult the instructions that come with the drive for any specific settings the manufacturer recommends. Most current BIOS chips and hard drives permit you to select "Auto Detect," which tells the computer to query the drive to determine proper settings.

The final step is to partition and format the drive. If you have purchased a complete hard drive kit, the sort typically sold at computer retail outlets, you should find a diskette with a configuration program; examples include Maxtor's MaxBlast Plus and Ontrack's Disk Manager or the EZ-BIOS utility. These sorts of program will make the necessary work-arounds if your system BIOS or interface cannot work with the large capacity of modern drives and otherwise automate the process for you.

If you don't install one of these BIOS extensions, your hard drive capacity may be limited to 8.4 GB.

If you have an up-to-date BIOS, you can choose to use the DOS and Windows utilities FDISK and FORMAT, respectively, to partition and then format your hard drive.

One way for an experienced PC upgrader to save a bit of money is to purchase a "bare" drive; manufacturers sell these drives in large quantities to PC makers and resellers. They lack fancy packaging and often come without cables, rails, and configuration programs. You can purchase the cables and rails separately and do without the configuration program, or go to the drive maker's Internet web page and download a copy from there.

About Partition Size

Current motherboards include a system BIOS that permits use of hard drives of 40 GB and larger without modification in combination with Windows 95 Service Release 2, Windows 98, or Windows 2000.

An older BIOS and operating systems released before Windows 95 Service Release 2 may not work with drives larger than 8.4 GB. Very old BIOS chips are even more limited.

Hard drive makers have managed to find ways to work around these limitations with software programs that fool the system into believing that one physical hard drive is actual two or more drives; they're called *logical drives*, meaning that their presence—or lack of physical presence, to be precise—makes sense to the BIOS and the microprocessor.

When you use the configuration software supplied with the hard drive, it should inform you whether the BIOS will support the drive as a single large partition or whether you'll have to use the supplied software to augment the BIOS and subdivide the drive into several smaller partitions.

(There's the matter of personal preference. I don't like having a single large partition on my hard drives, even though my current machines permit this. I like to set up one partition for the operating system and applications, a second partition for data, and a third partition for special projects such as temporary storage of images or audio files. You should set up your hard drive in whatever way makes sense to you.)

Upgrading to Ultra ATA/66

Most current motherboards now come with an Ultra ATA/66 adapter built into the motherboard, but you can upgrade an older PCI bus motherboard with an ATA/66 controller, like the one shown in Figure 4.16. This adapter, sold by SIIG, offers high-speed data transfer up to 66 MB per second, with support for drive capacities up to 128 GB and backward support for current IDE and ATAPI devices.

Figure 4.16

The device is a plug-and-play adapter that adds a dual-channel ATA/66 controller to Pentium-class computers. It fully supports the Ultra ATA/66 specifications, achieving burst data transfer rates of up to 66 MB per second, and supports drive capacities up to 128 GB. Just as with an onboard Ultra ATA/66 controller, it is also fully backward-compatible with earlier IDE specifications including Ultra ATA/33, EIDE/Fast ATA-2, IDE, and ATAPI devices.

An Ultra ATA/66 adapter card.

The add-in card coexists with onboard IDE ports, adding as many as four more IDE or ATAPI devices.

Troubleshooting a Hard Drive Installation

Here are a few troubleshooting tips on hard drive installation.

THE PC DOES NOT DETECT THE PRESENCE OF A NEW HARD DRIVE

1. Check to be certain that data and power cables are correctly oriented and fully inserted into cables on the drive and on the port on the motherboard or adapter card. If there is no power, the drive won't spin, something you may be able to notice with careful listening.

2. Determine if the drive has been properly set as a master or slave and that the corresponding jumper settings have been set on the drive.

3. Verify that the system BIOS has been set to recognize the drive; most modern BIOS chipsets will work with an Autoselect setting. The BIOS may also have to be instructed to look for hard drives on particular chains of the IDE port: the primary or secondary chain, and the master or slave device on each chain.

4. The drive must be partitioned and then formatted either by using an automatic configuration program supplied by the manufacturer or manually by using the FDISK and FORMAT programs. If you intend for the hard drive to boot the system, the formatting command must have specified that system tracks be copied to the drive.

5. On some occasions, certain devices will not work well together on the same cable or on the same port. IDE systems usually have a primary and secondary port, with a master and slave connector on each cable. Try changing the drive to work with a different cable or port.

PROBLEMS THAT ARISE DURING FDISK PARTITIONING   The drive's master boot record (MBR) may be corrupted. Check with the manufacturer of the drive for the availability of a utility that will restore, repair, or remove the MBR before partitioning.

THE PC HANGS DURING THE BOOT-UP PROCESS

1. The system BIOS may have a problem with the settings for the new drive's capacity or cylinder information. Verify the settings and try again.

2. On most drives, you can require the BIOS to use specific settings rather than the Autodetect option. Consult the instruction manual for your hard drive to determine the settings you should input on the BIOS set-up screen. The manual may also tell you to change a jumper on the hard drive to inform the IDE circuitry to use a cylinder limitation setting rather than Autodetect.

Installing a CD-ROM or DVD-ROM

CDs came to computers from the world of home audio. Instead of 60 minutes of Britney Spears, on a personal computer the small plastic discs can hold a whopping 650 MB of data.

Figure 4.17

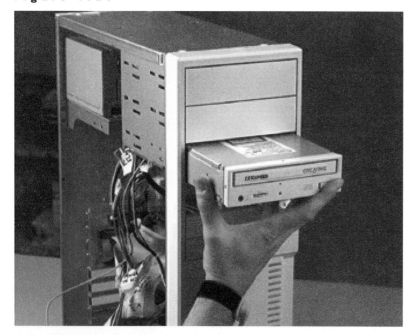

A CD-ROM installed through the front of the case.

In this section, all of the instructions for installation of a CD-ROM also apply to CD-R, CD-RW, and DVD-ROM drives. DVD devices may also require connection to a separate MPEG decoder card sold with the drive; newer and faster PCs are capable of decoding MPEG information using software and the PC's own CPU.

Because CD-ROMs require access to the outside of the case to allow disks to be inserted or taken out, they generally are installed or removed through the front of the case in a 5 1/4-inch bay, as seen in Figure 4.17.

If you're removing an older CD-ROM for an upgrade, you'll need to remove one to four screws that hold the CD-ROM in its bay. Label connectors and cables before you disconnect them; remove the power cable, the data cable, and the audio cable that runs to a sound card. Then slide the old drive out. Make note of any settings on the back of the device; unless you change its position on the cable or connect to a secondary port, your new CD-ROM will require the same master or slave setting as the one it replaces.

The rear of this new 52X CD-ROM, seen in Figure 4.18, is typical of most such devices. From left to right, Figure 4.18 shows the connectors for the digital audio, analog audio, CS/SL/MA block, host interface, power, and test and special features.

Figure 4.18

Connectors and jumpers on a CD-ROM.

Digital audio is used for output to certain sound cards and other audio devices.

Analog audio is used for output to most sound cards.

The *CS/SL/MA block* is a jumper block where the user designates the type of data cable employed in the connection. CS, not often used, indicates use of a Cable Select wire that determines master or slave status for a device. A jumper placed across the SL pins designates the device as a slave and across the MA block as master. Some CD-ROMs have a default setting (usually slave) that is in effect unless another option is chosen with jumpers. Be sure to consult the instruction manual that comes with the drive.

The *host interface* is where the data cable from the motherboards's IDE controller is attached. The designation of pins 1 and 2 and of 39 and 40 help you install the cable properly. There's also a notch at the top of the connector that mates to a protruding piece on the cable connector.

Netxt is the connector for *power*, marked with 5- and 12-volt pins and two ground pins. The power cable will only fit into the connector in the proper orientation.

One some devices, one more set of jumpers can be used for *testing* and for activation or deactivation of certain functions. Consult the instruction manual for details.

The four screws on the side of the CD-ROM allow it to be fixed in place in a drive bay of various designs. In most installations, just two screws—preferably one on each side of the drive—are sufficient to hold the drive in place.

The CD's audio output needs to be connected to the corresponding input on your machine's sound card. Many current sound cards come packaged with an audio cable, but in some instances you'll have to purchase (or construct from spare parts) a cable that works with your particular drive and card. Consult the instruction manuals for the drive and your sound card for details.

The default setting for a CD-ROM is as the slave device on an IDE chain, which is appropriate if the CD-ROM is connected to the primary IDE channel and the hard drive is configured as the master device. Configuring a hard drive secondary to a slower CD-ROM will slow down the hard drive's operations. However, you can make the CD-ROM the master device on the secondary IDE channel.

Figure 4.19

Internal connectors on a sound card.

You'll also need to connect the CD-ROM to your system's sound card using an audio cable. Most current CD-ROMs and sound cards work with a standard cable that is usually part of the CD-ROM package. In some cases, however, you'll have to purchase or make your own cable based on insructions in the CD-ROM or sound card manual. The internal connectors on a current sound card are shown in Figure 4.19.

Windows 95 or 98 will automatically recognize most current CD-ROMs the first time you turn on the system and install proper drivers from the Windows set or from a driver disk supplied by the CD-ROM maker.

If you're among the dwindling few running an older version of Windows or even DOS, you'll need to install Microsoft's CD-ROM extensions program, MSCDEX.EXE, into the start-up file for your computer. Consult the instruction manual for the CD-ROM for details or contact the maker's technical support line for specific instructions and settings for the command.

The new 52X CD-ROM is installed and running, as seen in Figure 4.20.

Keep in mind that speed claims for CD-ROMs are sometimes a bit on the fanciful side. Your actual throughput is determined by a number of factors, including rotational speed, buffer size, and the nature of the data on the disk. A 52X drive is surely faster than a 12X drive, but in most situations the difference is less than the fourfold boost you might expect.

By the way, high-speed CDs are noticeably more noisy when they first spin up a disk for access. They may also generate more heat than slower drives, something you should consider in planning for cooling of the case.

The new CD-ROM in place.

CD-R and CD-RW devices install in the same way as standard read-only CD-ROMs. You'll also find a range of external CD devices, such as the Imation CD-R shown in Figure 4.21, that connect to a SCSI or USB port. Another means to attach an external drive is through a parallel port, although throughput speed is much less with this sort of connection.

You will need to install software that controls the writing of information to the disks. One popular software application is Adaptec's Direct CD, shown in Figure 4.22.

Follow the instructions that come with your CD-R or CD-RW for installation of the software.

Many sellers of CD-R and CD-RW hardware package compo-

An external SCSI CD-ROM.

nents from various sources; they may sell their product under a generic name such as "52-X CD-ROM" or "8 × 20 CD-R" without making it obvious who manufactures the drive itself. Examine the drive before you install it to see if you can determine the maker and model number; if you can't find it on the device, call customer support and ask for this information. Then record what you've learned in the manual for the device for future reference.

Be cautious with using third-party CD-recording software; not all such software is compatible with all drives. Even if you install the software that comes with your drive, be wary of future updates to that software. Be sure any enhancements are appropriate for your particular model of drive.

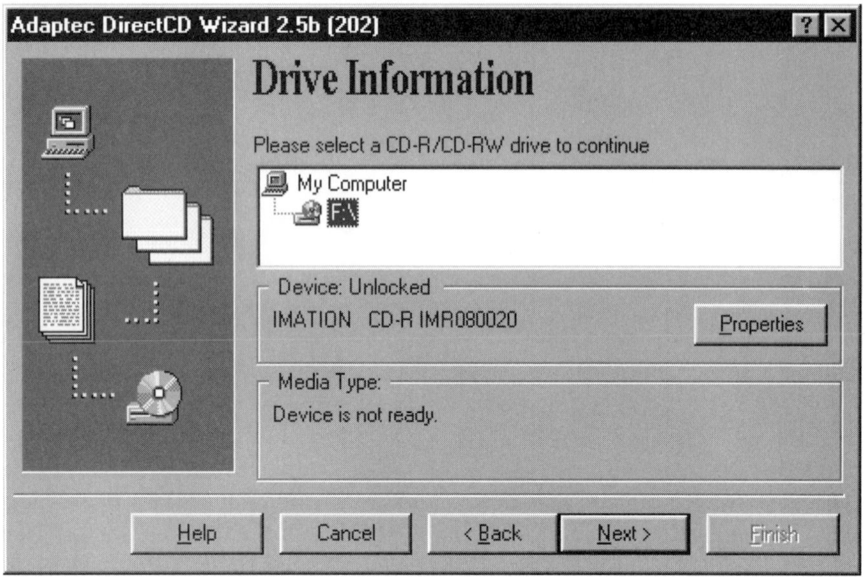

Figure 4.22

Direct CD software.

CHAPTER 5

Removable Storage

Project 2: Zip Drive, Superdisk, Tape Backup

The more important the work you do on your PC, the more you need some way to back up your data. Although computers and their components have become more and more reliable over the years, it is not a question of *whether* your PC or its hard drive will die, only a matter of *when*.

Early users made backups of their data by printing out copies of everything they were working on. The next step in the backup process was a slow and laborious copy to floppy disks; files that were larger than a disk's capacity had to be split across multiple disks where possible.

The modern era began with the arrival of large-capacity removable disks of various designs. As with other pieces of PC equipment, they have become faster, larger, and less expensive over time.

Any current backup system is better than none. Spend the time to consider your work habits, the type and size of files you create, and, perhaps most importantly, whether you will need to interchange backup media among other machines in your home or office or will need to ship copies of files by mail or courier.

Here is a selection of some current options for backup, along with my view of their utility; you may see things differently if your operations are different from mine.

ZIP DRIVES   The original version of this drive stored 100 MB of data on a special floppy disk roughly the same size as a $3^1/_2$-inch floppy disk but was not interchangeable with that older, slower, and much less capacious technology. The Zip 100 has a data-transfer rate of 1.4 MB per second and an access time of 29 milliseconds. The more recent version of the drive is the Zip 250, which, as its name suggests, can hold 250 MB of information. These drives can also read and write earlier 100-MB cartridges.

With the installation of Iomega's software drivers, Zip devices are recognized by Windows as if they were a regular disk in your system. Zip drives are available as internal IDE devices or as SCSI, USB, or a slower parallel port model. The drives sell for about $100 to $200, depending on capacity and connection; cost per megabyte of storage is about 10 cents. Other devices have come along that are larger and faster. The main advantage of using a Zip drive is their ubiquity; if you need to send a disk to another user, there is a good chance their machine will have a Zip drive.

SUPERDISK DRIVES   Imation's SuperDisk LS-120 technology uses a special type of $3^1/_2$-inch disk that can hold as much as 120 MB of data. The drives can also read and write to standard 1.44-MB floppy disks, making them useable as a replacement for ordinary $3^1/_2$-inch drives. An internal drive costs about $100, with a cost per megabyte of about 10 cents. The ability to use original $3^1/_2$-inch disks is an advantage, but Superdisks are much less common than Zip drives.

The LS in LS-120 stands for laser servo, a technology that uses a laser to determine position and control a motor to precisely position the read–write head over the proper track on a disk, which increases the data track density of a standard $3^1/_2$-inch disk from 135 to 2,490 tracks per inch.

JAZ DRIVES   Iomega's Jaz drives store a whopping 2 GB of data on a removable cartridge; the original version of the drive stored 1 GB. The original model transferred data at a respectable 6.6 MB per second, with an access time of 12 milliseconds, roughly comparable to an unextraordinary hard drive; the 2-GB model is slightly faster than the original. Jaz drives require a SCSI interface. The 2-GB drive sells for about $530; cost per megabyte for that model is about 6 cents. Although the Jaz drives are attractive, they are not as common as Zip drives and may present a problem if you need to ship a disk to another user.

ORB DRIVES   A competitor to the Jaz drive, Castlewood's Orb drives are fast, capacious, and inexpensive. The 2.2-GB drive sells for about $200 in EIDE, SCSI, and USB versions; cartridges are very inexpensive, with a cost per megabyte of about 1.5 cents. The disadvantage of the Orb is that it is a relative newcomer in an already established market and there is no way to predict its staying power. The drives are even less common than Jaz drives.

CD-R AND CD-RW DRIVES   Since they were first introduced, writeable (CD-R) and rewriteable (CD-RW) drives have become easier and faster and, recently, much less expensive to purchase. The installation of an internal CD-ROM was discussed in Chapter 4.

Drives can store as much as 650 MB of information, and current models produce disks that can be read in any equally current CD-ROM drive; you can even use the disks on Apple Macintosh systems. The difference between CD-Rs and CD-RWs is that CD-RWs can erase and rewrite on the same disk many times, whereas CD-R disks can only be written to once. Some CD-RWs produce disks that cannot be reliably read in standard CD-ROMS; investigate compatibility before buying one. Drives sell for about $200 to $400, depending on speed, and cost per megabyte is about a tenth of a penny for a write-once disk or half a penny for rewriteable disks.

TAPE BACKUPS   These devices can backup an entire hard disk; capacities for consumer-level tape drives reach to 50 GB. They are generally easy to use, depending on the particular software you use to manage them. They are, however, very slow in comparison with the other mechanisms because of the way they record information in serial fashion down the length of a tape. Think of the difference between moving a needle to any track of a record album (remember those?) compared with having to fast-forward your way to a particular scene in a long video tape. Tape drives are relatively inexpensive, about $200 to $300, and tape cartridges range in cost per megabyte from about a third of a cent to a penny.

My Backup Strategy

And so you might wonder which type of backup device a supposed expert in the field uses in his office? Well, the answer is almost all of them.

I use a 100-MB Zip drive to send files to some of the publishers I work with because the device is very common in that industry. I also use the Zip drive to make quick backups of projects I worked on over the course of a single day.

I use a CD-R to make archival copies of large files and entire projects. I also use CD-Rs to send files to people who don't have Zip drives.

I use a 30-GB tape drive to make backups of my entire data drive on a Monday–Wednesday–Friday schedule. The tape would allow me to reconstruct the drive in the case of a catastrophic failure.

Installing an Internal Zip Drive

An internal Zip drive needs access from the outside of the case just like a floppy disk drive. Within our demonstration PC, it installs in the drive cage, as seen in Figure 5.1.

Figure 5.1

A Zip drive installed in an internal drive bay.

Many current PC cases come with only a single 3$\frac{1}{2}$-inch opening on the front, intended for use by a floppy disk drive. In that situation, you'll need to remove a plastic or metal bezel from the front of the case, as shown in Figure 5.2, to allow access to the Zip drive once it is installed.

You can also install a 3$\frac{1}{2}$-inch device like a Zip drive in a 5$\frac{1}{4}$-inch bay; you'll need to use a mounting kit with conversion brackets and a converter for the bezel at the front of the case, as shown in Figure 5.3. If the mounting kit does not come with your drive, you can purchase one from most computer supply stores.

Before screwing the Zip drive in place, check to see if you need to make any changes to the jumpers on the back panel. Zip drives come with a default setting as a slave device on an IDE chain; you'll need to install a jumper to designate the drive as a master or to use a Cable Select connection, as shown in Figure 5.4. Iomega provides a jumper diagram on the drive itself, a thoughtful touch. Pin 1 on the data cable is marked, and there is also a notch to ensure proper configuration. Figure 5.5 shows the completed subassembly, with Zip and floppy drives slid back in place.

Installing an Internal Superdisk Drive

One of several competitors to the Zip drive is Imation's Superdisk, which packs 120 MB of data on special LS-120 floppy disks, but can also read and write to standard 1.44-MB floppies, allowing the drive to replace a basic floppy disk drive. Internal IDE versions install in the same manner as a Zip drive.

A good way to maximize storage without giving up an extra disk bay, the Superdisk's only significant drawback is that its acceptance has not been as widespread as the Zip. If you plan to share disks with others, you'll have to make certain they have a Superdisk drive available. Figure 5.6 shows an external unit that connects to a parallel port.

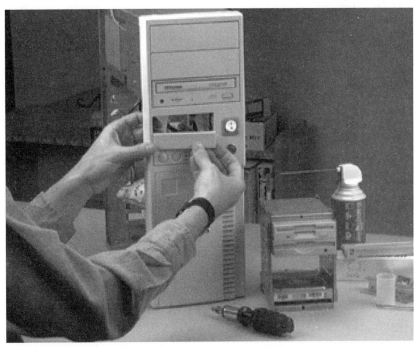

Figure 5.2

Removing the bezel to make room for a new drive.

Onstream Echo Tape Backup

An example of a modern, convenient tape backup device is Onstream's Echo SC30e external SCSI model, shown in Figure 5.7.

The Echo is capable of storing as much as 30 GB of compressed data on a single 15-GB cartridge. Onstream also offers a 50-GB model and variants that connect to computers through a USB port or the parallel port. The huge storage capacity not only allows you to back up all of the data on your machine, it also permits an ongoing incremental backup that stores all saved versions of a single file. If, for example, you decide that you'd like to

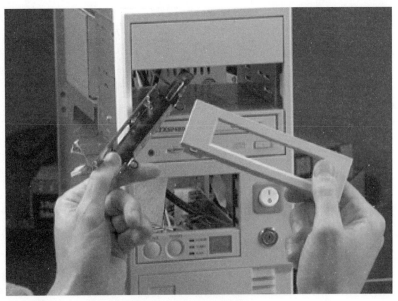

Figure 5.3

Converting a 5¹/₄-inch opening for a 3¹/₂-inch device.

Figure 5.4

Jumpers on the rear of a Zip drive.

resurrect a version of the file from a few hours or a few days past, Onstream's Echo software can retrieve it.

The drive is based on advanced digital recording technology, a variable-speed recording method that reads and writes eight channels of data simultaneously. The tape includes an embedded servo on the tape cartridge for accuracy, and the eight heads allow the controller to spatially distribute error correction code, thereby improving speed and reliability.

Transfer speeds are as fast as 2 MB per second, fast enough to use the cartridge for some streaming video or audio files. The cost of a cartridge works out to a very reasonable $1 or so per compressed gigabyte, or a tenth of a cent per megabyte.

Used as a background backup device, Onstream's Echo software, shown in Figure 5.8, can be instructed to automatically make copies of all files or of new and modified files on a regular schedule. You can also instruct the software to make backups on demand.

Figure 5.5

A drive bay with Zip and floppy drives.

The Onstream Echo drive is assigned a drive letter, allowing you to use it just like any other removable drive on your system, including dragging and dropping files to it.

The external SCSI version of the Onstream tape drive can also be used with a Mac system, with the addition of a Macintosh backup software application.

Figure 5.6

An external Superdisk drive.

Figure 5.7

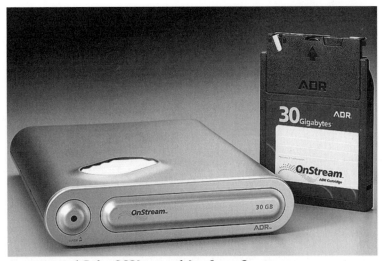

An external Echo SCSI tape drive from Onstream.

Figure 5.8

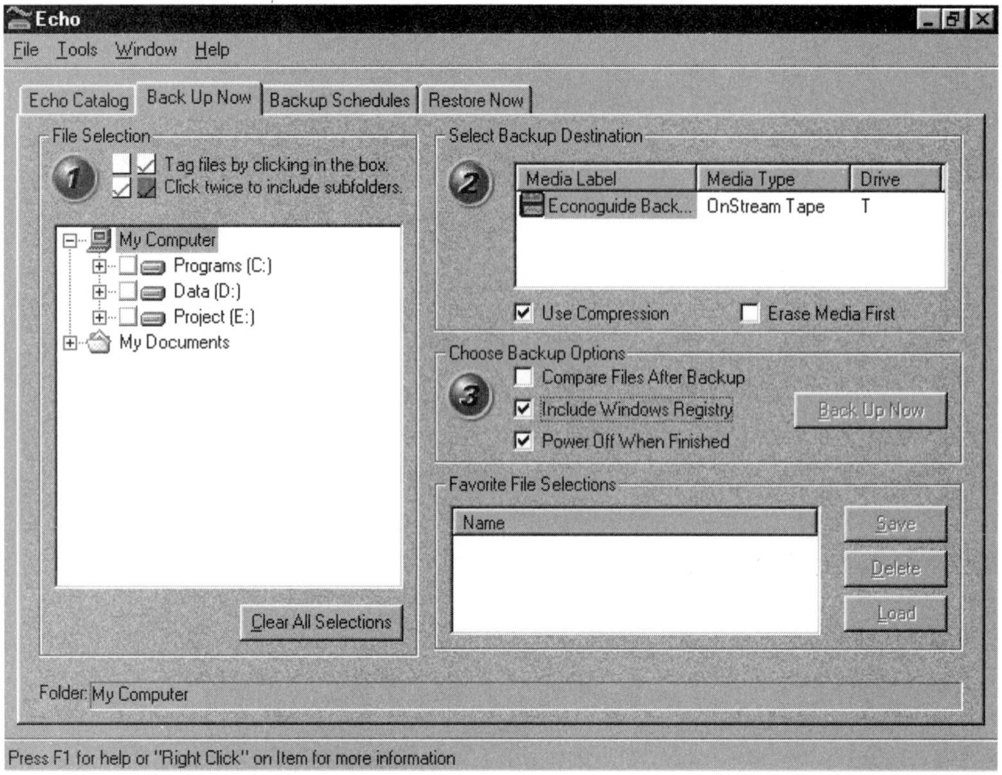

Echo backup software for a tape device.

CHAPTER 6

Memory

Project 3: Adding RAM

Adding memory to your computer is one of the simplest, most cost-effective ways to improve its speed and ease of use. How much memory do you need? Although you can get away with a bit less, in my opinion modern machines running current operating systems such as Windows 98 and large office suites should have at least 32 MB of RAM. More RAM is always better than less. All the PCs in my office have at least 64 MB; production machines used to process graphics have at least 128 MB.

More RAM allows the CPU to handle multiple tasks without having to immediately record every change to the hard disk. Additional memory is also especially useful for graphics-intensive programs including photo editors, illustration software, and many games.

Your system's RAM is the working space for the computer, a place where data and programs are spread out and available to the processor. It's called random access memory because the computer can jump directly to any place as if it were reaching into a huge desktop to grab a piece of a jigsaw puzzle.

Compare this to disk storage, which is like a huge record player with information stored in its tracks. With the aid of a fast-moving magnetic head, the disk controller can move to a particular spot to grab information, but the system will have to wait for that head to get into position and for the spinning disk to turn far enough so that the data is beneath the head.

Over the relatively short history of the PC, there have been dozens of memory architectures, technologies, chip carriers, and sockets. Memory technology, like most everything else in computers, has advanced rapidly to become faster, larger, and less expensive. (More so than with other components, memory has become a generic component that is sometimes subject to wild swings in pricing and availability due to supply and demand; in 1999, for example, memory prices spiked upward sharply after an earthquake in Taiwan damaged factories there. Prices began to settle back to relative bargain status within a year.)

The first PCs used small and somewhat unreliable individual chips that mounted in rows of sockets on the motherboard. The next step in the progress of machines brought memory cards that held large quantities— 640 KB was considered a huge block of memory in the early days of the PC—on a card that plugged into the bus.

More modern machines, the ones covered in this book for upgrade projects, use 72-pin SIMMs and, more recently, 168-pin DIMMs to hold RAM. A typical machine today uses 64 MB or more of memory, with some graphics workstations holding 1 GB or more.

When PCs were first introduced, designers were very concerned about errors that might be introduced by flaky memory chips, and not without good reason. Early users could expect a few memory-related failures a day.

Designers worked to come up with an error-checking scheme; the one that was used in the original PCs was called *parity checking*. For every eight bits (one byte) of memory, the system had a ninth bit that recorded whether the sum of the other eight bits was odd or even. If the value of the parity bit did not match the calculated value of the byte of memory when it was checked, an error code was generated and the system usually ground to a halt. There was no correction of the error and to make things worse there was an inherent flaw in the concept: if an even number of bits within a byte went bad, they would cancel each other out in the parity checking.

Parity checking was primitive and added some expense to the system for the extra bits of memory and the chips to control the scheme.

Virtually all of the machines covered in this book, especially those using DIMMs, have dispensed with parity checking, and you should not purchase and use parity memory. However if your system does need the ninth bit, you will need to search out this type of RAM.

There are dozens of possible combinations of RAM types; your best bet is to call the manufacturer or consult the instruction manual for your motherboard or system, or the build list for your computer when you ordered it, to determine the type of memory in use.

If in doubt, open the covers of the PC and examine the RAM in place on the motherboard. Write down the markings on the SIMMs or DIMMs you find installed.

Once you have all the information, purchasing memory is simple. I'd suggest you call one of the mail order memory vendors or consult an online ordering page for the best prices and widest selection of modules.

In general, you should avoid mixing types and speeds of RAM. If the modules you purchase are not an exact match for older memory already in place, consult the instruction manual or ask the vendor for advice about whether, as is usually the case, the faster modules should be in the first bank on the motherboard.

How Much Memory Do You Have?

There's no need to count the chips in the memory sockets to determine how much memory is already installed in your computer.

The quickest way is to watch the report on the screen of your computer as it boots up when you first turn on the power. Nearly all BIOS programs include a memory test that is displayed on screen.

If you're running Windows 95 or 98, you can check on memory resources by going to Start/Settings/Control Panel and then double-clicking the System icon. Choose the Performance tab. You'll see a report like the one shown in Figure 6.1.

In addition to a report on the total amount of memory in the system, in this case 128 MB, you'll also learn how much of that memory is free for use under Windows. If the amount is 25 percent or less, Windows is sure to be operating much slower than it should because it will have to rely on swap files on hard disks for some of its own code and those of applications.

You can also obtain a report on system resources from within most Microsoft Office applications by clicking on Help, the option that tells you about the application you're within, and then on the System Info button.

Similar information is also available from within utility programs such as Norton SystemWorks.

How Much Memory Do You Need?

Figure 6.1

Control Panel memory report.

More memory is better than less. Beyond this maxim, the precise amount of memory needed for a particular system varies. In my opinion, a basic Windows 95 or 98 system should have a minimum of 32 MB of RAM.

If you're going to multitask, that is, have more than one program open and running at one time, I'd boost that minimum to 64 MB. If you're going to use image-editing programs like Adobe Photoshop, I'd go up one or two notches to 96 or 128 MB. Graphic artists often feel the need for much more.

Just a few years ago, numbers like these would have seemed outrageous. To begin with, RAM was expensive. Beyond that, operating systems and microprocessors were not well suited to managing that much memory. Today, however, processors in the Pentium II and Pentium III families and compatible CPUs from AMD work just fine with large amounts of memory. In addition, prices of RAM have settled into a range of about $1 per megabyte, an amazing bargain when viewed from a historical perspective.

Counting Memory

Memory capacity is measured in bytes, which are in turn each made up of eight bits. Eight bits of binary code is equal to 1,024; eight bytes of binary code equals 1,024 bytes.

Just to make things confusing, computer specifications use the Greek prefixes of kilo, mega, giga, and tera in front of measurements based on binary math. For example, kilo means 1,000, but as used in kilobyte, it means 1,024 bytes; similarly, mega means 1,000,000, but as a binary representation, it means 1,048,576 (Table 6.1).

Table 6.1
Binary Abbreviations

Abbreviation	Meaning	Value as a Decimal Number
Kb	Kilobit	1,024 bits
KB	Kilobyte	1,024 bytes
Mb	Megabit	1,048,576 bits
MB	Megabyte	1,048,576 bytes
Gb	Gigabit	1,073,741,824 bits
GB	Gigabyte	1,073,741,824 bytes
Tb	Terabit	1,099,511,627,776 bits
TB	Terabyte	1,099,511,627,776 bytes

If you are running Windows 95 or 98, you can take a quick measure of the amount of memory in your system by clicking Start/Settings/Control Panel and then double-clicking the System icon. Choose the Performance tab for a report on the total amount of memory in the system and on the percentage of memory free for use. Load up your standard group of applications and check the amount of memory for the group. Any amount below 50 percent indicates a system that is laboring. If the figure is below 25 percent, you have a critical need for more memory, at least with the current group of applications running.

Today's DIMMs are more reliable than any of the previous technologies, and the chips they hold are less likely to fail than the module itself or the socket on the motherboard. You can safely purchase as large a module as you need. Purchasing a single large module will save a bit of money over two or more smaller ones and will leave room for future expansion.

Preparing for New Memory

The procedure for adding either a SIMM or DIMM to your PC's motherboard is very similar to adding RAM.

The first step is to find out the specifications of your motherboard: does it use SIMMs or DIMMs (or both, as was seen in some transitional motherboards as technologies evolved). Does it use standard 3.3-volt memory or another voltage? Does the system require EDO or SDRAM technologies?

If your current machine uses speedy SDRAM modules, you'll need to know whether your system bus runs at 100 MHz or 133 MHz. What refresh

A 64-MB RAM module for an older 66-MHz bus.

speed do the memory modules offer, and what are the speeds of any existing modules on the board? For older machines, you'll need to know whether the memory modules use parity checking or are nonparity devices.

Figure 6.2 shows a 66-MHz DIMM from Kingston in its antistatic case next to the demonstration PC.

Before all this jargon gives you a headache, you should be able to find all of the answers to your questions in the instruction manual for your PC; look for the specifications page or a section that deals with memory upgrades. You can also carefully remove the memory modules in the machine and bring them (packed properly) to a computer store or record all of the information on them and call a mail order or Internet memory vendor.

Take great care to guard against mixing incompatible types of memory in one system. Wherever possible, match existing modules. If you must mix types, consult the instruction manual for advice on where to place faster modules; for example, on many machines, the faster memory should be in bank 0.

Many users will end up in a situation where most or all of their SIMM or DIMM slots are filled, but with modules that add up to an inadequate amount of memory. For example, an older machine with just two DIMM slots may have a pair of 8-MB modules. There's really no choice here but to remove these perfectly good but undersized old modules and replace them with newer, larger ones.

Don't throw away the old memory because you may be able to sell the modules to brokers who recycle them to other users, or you may want to donate them to a school or community center. You can find the names of brokers in the back pages of some computer magazines.

Installing Memory

To install memory to your computer, think like a surgeon: you want to prepare the operating field to be as clean and safe as possible and give yourself as much working room and light as possible.

Turn off the power switch and unplug your computer before removing the cover.

I strongly suggest you use an antistatic strap or pad to protect both your computer and the memory you will be adding. If you don't have an antistatic device, make sure to touch an unpainted, grounded object before touching the memory or your computer.

Locate the memory expansion slots or sockets on the motherboard. Check the computer or motherboard instruction manual to see if there is any requirement that the sockets be filled in a particular order, or if they must be filled in pairs. If you don't have any open sockets, you'll have to remove one or more of the lower-capacity memory SIMMs or DIMMs to make room for new ones.

(You may be able to sell used memory chips to companies that recycle the devices. Some computer stores sell SIMM or DIMM "doublers" that permit you to install two modules in the same slot. Take care to ensure that any such device fits in your system and is of acceptable quality.)

Installing a 72-Pin SIMM

Figure 6.3

Locate the positioning "key" on the module, a rounded notch, visible in Figure 6.3. A matching bridge on the socket ensures that the module can only be inserted in the proper direction. Do not attempt to force a module; doing so can damage the module and crack the motherboard.

Insert the module at a slight angle.

When the module is fully inserted, rotate it upward in the socket until the clips at both ends of the socket click into place.

A 72-pin SIMM installs in its socket.

Installing a 168-Pin DIMM

Locate the key on the module and match it to the corresponding keys on the socket, as shown in Figure 6.4. Don't force the module.

Figure 6.4

Lining up the key slots on a 168-pin DIMM.

EDO and SDRAM 168-pin DIMMs appear very similar but are electrically incompatible. Both modules have an extra notch near the number 1 position. The SDRAM notch is in a slightly different location, making it difficult but not impossible to force one or the other type of DIMM module into the wrong connector.

Most 168-pin DIMMs have plastic ejector tabs on each end, like those shown in Figure 6.5; these are used only if you need to remove a module. Press down on the tab to pop up the module from its socket.

Your system may also have several other types of memory that can be upgraded for better performance. The older Microstar motherboard, shown in Figure 6.6, has a slot for installation of a cache memory module just above the microprocessor socket. Cache helps the CPU zip through complex and repetitive instructions by placing a small amount of very high-speed memory alongside the CPU.

Figure 6.5

Ejector tabs on a DIMM socket.

Primary cache, also called level 1, L1, or internal cache, is usually part of the microprocessor itself. Secondary cache, also called level 2 or L2 cache, can reside on the CPU package or on a separate block on the motherboard.

Other blocks of memory can be found on many graphics cards and on some sound cards.

Consult the instruction manuals for your system and devices to see if they are upgradeable by the user and for specifications on the type of memory you'll need.

Figure 6.6

Socket for cache memory on an older motherboard.

CHAPTER 7

Input and Output

Project 4: Serial, Parallel, USB, SCSI Ports, FireWire, and Network Interface Cards

The basic input and output ports for the PC, from its birth, have been the parallel and serial port, and in many ways they have remained the backbone of data transport.

Serial ports are used mostly for modems, mice, and some specialized communications devices.

Parallel ports work well for short-distance transfer of large amounts of information. As such, they are commonly used for printers and as one interconnection path for devices such as scanners and external CD-ROMs and hard drives.

In recent years, the serial interface has been extended and expanded with various versions of the SCSI interface and the more recent USB.

USB transfers data at speeds of up to 6 MB per second, which is 20 times faster than a parallel port and 75 times the rate of a serial port. On the horizon is USB 2.0, which promises blazing speed.

The current speed champion for input and output (I/O) is Ultra2 Wide SCSI, which operates as fast as 80 MB per second, connecting as many as 15 devices on a chain of cables that can extend as far as 12 meters (about 37 feet). On the horizon is Ultra160 SCSI, which is capable of transferring data at a rate of 160 MB per second.

Basic Fast SCSI runs at 10 MB per second with as many as 7 devices on the chain. In between are Ultra SCSI (20 MB per second and 7 devices) and Ultra Wide SCSI (40 MB per second and 15 devices).

One other I/O facility is a network interface card, which allows two or more PCs to form a consortium to share data, hardware, and sometimes programs. I'll discuss the hardware side of networking in this chapter; the software side, although relatively easy to configure, is beyond the scope of this book.

Parallel Ports

The parallel port was originally designed to rapidly transmit data from the computer to a printer, a one-way communication. Over the years it has been upgraded to a high-speed version, capable of bidirectional communication. The bidirectional wiring allows many interesting facilities: a printer can communicate back to the computer to report that it is out of paper or ink, for example. Designers have used this path to devices in ways not envisioned when the port was designed: there are now scanners, modems, and CD-ROMs that send and receive their information through the parallel port.

Within a computer, the bus that interconnects the major components is a high-speed multilane superhighway of 8, 16, or 32 wires. In the original PC design, one byte (eight bits) moved along in parallel spread across the eight wires of the bus.

Over the course of the history of PCs, this bus has widened to two bytes (16 bits over 16 wires) and four bytes (32 bits over 32 wires.) When the data is sent to a parallel port for output to a printer or other device, the computer words are chopped up into eight-bit pieces and sent through the port; in theory, a parallel port can be eight times as fast as a serial port because the bits move alongside each other instead of one after the other.

Over the years, there have been four generations of parallel port design, each improving on the previous in speed and capability. The most current machines include ports that support all of the capabilities.

The original parallel port was *unidirectional*; it was sometimes called a *Centronics* port, named after the manufacturer of a particular printer that was common in the early days of computers. This specification had a top speed of about 50 Kbps and permitted only one-way flow of data from the computer to a printer.

The next step was *bidirectional*, which permitted communication back from the printer or other device to the PC and also boosted the maximum transfer rate to 300 Kbps.

Modern machines offer an *enhanced parallel port* (EPP), which boasts speeds of as much as 1 Mbps. The arrival of this protocol allowed use of the parallel port for devices including external hard drives and backup units, scanners, and other devices.

The *extended capabilities port* (ECP) extended the previous two-way facilities for more sophisticated external peripherals.

Check the specifications of any device you hope to attach to your PC. Advanced devices almost always require an EPP or ECP.

If your older machine has only a bidirectional port or an antique unidirectional port, you'll need to upgrade. Fortunately, this is a relatively simple task on most machines; you'll find a range of expansion cards that will upgrade older machines.

Installing a Parallel Port

You can add a current parallel port to a PCI system with an adapter card such as SIIG's single fast ECP/EPP parallel port, shown in Figure 7.1.

The adapter works with high-speed parallel devices including Zip and other removeable drives, scanners, printers, and some CD-R or CD-RWs. The plug-and-play device supports EPP/ECP bidirectional parallel port, and standard parallel port modes; configuration is made from within the Windows Control Panel.

Figure 7.1

PCI bus parallel port adapter.

Standard PC motherboards can support as many as three parallel ports, identified to the system as LPT1 through LPT3.

The basic parallel port can support only one device at a time, but many current peripherals allow a "pass-through" of the signal from one device to another. This should work well for devices that don't both require the system's attention at the same time. For example, a printer and a CD-ROM can share a parallel port in this way as long as you don't attempt to print from the contents of the CD-ROM. (To get around that particular problem, you could export data from the CD-ROM to a file on your hard drive and then print from there.)

Figure 7.2

High–IRQ parallel port for ISA bus.

Windows 95 and Windows 98 should automatically assign IRQs, I/O port addresses, and DMA channels to any ports in your system; you can also manually assign the ports under your system BIOS or within the System page of Control Panel in Windows. Each port needs its own resources, unduplicated by other devices.

For systems that don't have a PCI bus or where the PCI slots are all in use, you can add an ISA bus adapter with ports, such as SIIG's ISA single fast high-IRQ parallel port, shown in Figure 7.2.

As an ISA device this adapter is not plug-and-play, but the card is designed to work with standard and high IRQ settings to permit a wide range of configurations. Jumpers on the card are used to select from IRQ 5, 7, and 9 through 12 and from DMA channels 0, 1, and 3.

Serial Ports

The serial port was originally used for relatively slow and simple communication between a computer and a modem or mouse. Because of the single pipeline of the serial connection, in most cases only one device could use a port at a time. Nearly every PC includes two basic serial ports and sometimes more.

Picture this traffic jam for a moment: hundreds of thousands or even millions of bits of information per second speed along the 16 or 32 wires of a modern computer bus until they come to a serial port. There they have to be stored for a moment and put in line one behind the other for output. In addition, the system has to add special characters to the information to mark the beginning and end of each word of data so that it can be reassembled at the other end. Some forms of serial communication also send error detection and correction information along with the data.

Early computers were slow and worked in computer words of only four or eight bytes. Computer printers also were slow mechanical devices that struck characters one at a time like a typewriter or punched them out in dot-matrix form. Early modems were also very slow. Therefore serial ports were acceptable for use with most devices.

Modern computers, of course, are much faster. Most printers have moved from serial to the faster parallel ports. Today, serial ports are used mostly for modems, which send data across a phone line in character-by-character form. PCs also use serial ports for transmission of data from mice and some other input devices that don't require a great deal of speed.

The engine that chops up incoming parallel data from the bus and strings them together in serial fashion is the universal asynchronous receiver/transmitter, or UART (pronounced "you-art").

The original UART for PCs was called 8250 and is hopelessly out of date because it is unable to work with modems faster than 9,600 bps in an era of 56,000-bps devices. The next step up was the 16450, which was able to work at what is today a still poky 14,400 bps.

To work with current modems and other serial devices, your PC should have a UART in the 16550 family. These chips can move data as fast as 115,200 bps and offer other facilities that speed along the process of disassembling and reassembling bytes.

On older machines, the 8250 or 16450 UART was held in a socket and could be removed and replaced with a 16550 chip. Upgrading was as simple as pulling out the old chip from the motherboard and installing a new one.

On current machines, the UART may be soldered into a surface mount or incorporated into a chipset that integrates a number of features.

You can find out what kind of a UART is in your system by studying the instruction manual or by consulting some system utilities.

If the UART cannot be replaced on the motherboard or if you'd rather take another route, you can instead install an expansion card in the bus with a more current serial controller chip. These cards can disable and replace the existing serial ports, or they can install additional serial ports to your system.

There are also some specialized expansion cards for unusual communications needs using UARTs such as the 16750, which can work as fast as 921 Kbps, and the 16950, which offers a 128-byte buffer. These high-speed interfaces are typically used in scientific or electronic commerce applications.

Expansion cards can add one, two, or even four serial ports. Combination cards can also add a bidirectional parallel port for a second such interface or to upgrade an older and outdated parallel interface.

The original, slower serial ports are generally good enough for simple hardware such as a mouse.

The main reason to upgrade an outmoded serial port is to be able to work with a faster modem such as the current 56K devices. Instead of replacing an existing serial port or adding an expansion card, you can install a current internal modem card. These cards include their own 16550 or equivalent UART, and you may be able to keep existing serial ports in place.

Internal modems offer their own set of advantages and disadvantages when compared to external devices. On the plus side, they do not use up one of your existing serial ports and they are less expensive than external units. On the down side, they require their own IRQ and memory resource allocations, draw a bit of power and generate a bit of heat within the case, and lack external indicator lights and on–off switches.

Current PCs have 16 interrupts, numbered from 0 to 15. IRQs are channels used by devices to signal to the processor that they need attention. Memory addresses are a bit like postal codes: they identify the place where the system can find the door to a device for receiving or transmitting information.

Each serial port needs an IRQ and a memory address; although you can do so, in most situations you'll want to avoid changing the assignments of COM1 or COM2 because many software programs expect to find these devices at specific locations. However, COM3 and above can be assigned almost any IRQ and memory location.

In theory, Windows 95/98 and 2000 can automatically assign interrupts and memory addresses; if you're lucky, there's nothing for you to do but plug-and-play. In my experience, however you're likely to have to engage in at least a few rounds of "What's My Computer Line" before a new serial other than standard COM1 and COM2 is recognized and other devices in the system are shifted around to avoid conflicts.

To reassign a COM port under Windows 95/98, check current port settings from the Device Manager. Select Start, Settings, and then Control Panel. Click the System icon and then select the Device Manager tab. Click on the + mark next to Ports and examine the ports indicator.

If you see an exclamation mark within a yellow circle, Windows is reporting a possible conflict between devices. Double-click on the circle and then choose the Properties button and then the Resources tab. On the tab you'll find a report on Conflicting Devices from Windows, which should list devices that have resource conflicts.

Depending on the device and the driver supplied by the manufacturer, you should be able to unclick the Automatic Settings box on the tab and then manually reassign the IRQ, I/O port address, or both for one of the conflicting devices.

You can find a list of unused IRQs and I/O addresses by returning to the Device Manager and double-clicking Computer.

Installing a Serial Port

If you need to update an older serial port or install additional high-speed ports, you can install an adapter such as SIIG's PCI single fast 16550 serial port adapter, shown in Figure 7.3.

Figure 7.3

The PCI bus improves I/O access speed as much as eight times faster than existing ISA bus serial ports and supports baud rates of up to 460 Kbps.

A built-in 16-byte FIFO buffer dramatically increases data transmit/receive speed, especially in a multitasking environment under Windows. An IRQ sharing feature should eliminate most interrupt conflicts. Settings are made by using the device's driver and through the Windows Control Panel. This adapter adds a sin-

Serial port adapter card for the PCI bus.

Figure 7.4

High-IRQ serial port adapter card for the ISA bus.

gle 9-pin serial port; other similar devices add two or more ports.

For older systems with only ISA bus slots to spare, an adapter card such as SIIG's ISA single fast high-IRQ serial port, shown in Figure 7.4, delivers just what its name promises. The card adds a current 16550 UART, which supports data transfer rates of up to 115.2 Kbps.

The factory default setting for this card sets the single 9-pin serial port as COM2 and uses standard system resources of IRQ3 and a memory address of 2F8h. Two sets of jumpers on the card can be used to select COM3 or COM4 and choose among IRQs 3 through 5, 7, 9 through 12, and 15. Standard memory addresses are associated with whichever COM number you choose.

The Universal Serial Bus

In theory, the USB is the computer world's equivalent of sliced bread. It's markedly faster than a standard serial port, easy to configure, and compatible across the great PC/Mac divide.

To a great extent, USB has met its promise, although it was a bit late and buggy in its first implementation.

Today, you're able to find all manner of devices capable of using a USB connection: keyboards, mice, scanners, digital cameras, printers, modems, Ethernet adapters, hard disks, CD-ROMs, storage devices, and most everything else.

One vision of the future of the PC sees devices that are built around USB ports, dispensing with standard serial and parallel ports.

On a USB interface, data flows in a serial fashion (one bit behind the other) over simple wires, at speeds of up to 12 Mbps.

A major difference between USB and the original serial port is the ability of one USB port to support as many as 127 devices in an extended chain.

Devices can be plugged in or removed from the chain without rebooting the system. The USB devices themselves are a bit simpler because they can draw power from the same cable that connects them to the computer.

USB is what engineers call a master–slave design, with the PC controlling the flow of data. This allows slave devices (peripherals) to be simpler and less expensive. The transmission of power through the USB interface also simplifies the peripherals.

A USB system can include four types of devices: I/O devices, hubs, compound devices, and composite devices.

The *I/O device* is a peripheral by itself.

Hubs split USB ports into multiple branches. Under USB 1.0, hubs can be cascaded to a depth of five levels. (Although unpowered hubs are available, they're not recommended for systems with multiple hubs and devices.)

Compound devices are peripherals that include built-in hubs for further extension of the USB chain. For example, many USB monitors include connectors for keyboards and mice, simplifying the desktop landscape.

Composite devices combine several I/O functions in one peripheral, such as a combination modem and Ethernet interface.

On the PC, support for USB arrived with the B revision of Windows 95 and became fully integrated with Windows 98. The motherboard must also include USB circuitry, or you'll need to add an expansion card with USB ports. The standard implementation calls for two USB ports on a PC, although you can install additional ports with expansion cards.

Some older motherboards that were offered after the introduction of the technology but before devices arrived on the market offered USB circuitry but not a USB port. If you have one of these older motherboards, you need to purchase and install an adapter cable that connects to a connector on the motherboard and a bracket with USB ports, which installs in one of the openings on the back of the case.

You can connect a device directly to the USB port. However, most users will want to add a USB hub that splits off the data and power to several connectors. I have worked with hubs that offer two, four, and seven ports; you can also connect a line from a hub into another hub to further extend the USB chain.

A USB port provides 500 mA of power to devices; this is generally enough for one or two low-power devices such as keyboards or mice. If you will be connecting more than that number of devices or using peripherals with larger power demands, you'll want to use a powered hub that amplifies the current for devices.

The USB cable uses four wires: one each for sending and receiving data, one for power, and one for ground.

Engineers are already at work on USB 2.0, a specification that may run as much as 30 to 40 times as fast as the original interface when using the same devices. The goal is to maintain backward compatibility with older PCs and devices.

In Chapter 11, I'll upgrade an older motherboard to include a USB port and examine a range of USB devices.

SCSI Ports

The first significant improvement to the serial standard was the introduction of SCSI ports, which were derived from large mainframe and mini-computer technologies. SCSI, pronounced "skuzzy," is an acronym for a rarely used title: *small computer system interface.*

SCSI has gone through many improvements to its speed over the years; it's other advantage is the ability to work with as many as 15 devices on a single chain. SCSI ports and chains have often presented headaches in configuration of the PC and devices, although in more recent years companies such as Adaptec have offered sophisticated software utilities and drivers that make the set-up almost foolproof.

Unlike IDE devices, which put most of the logic on the controller on the motherboard or an adapter card, SCSI devices require management at both ends of the line: the controller and the device itself. This makes devices a bit more expensive to manufacture, but it allows the SCSI specification to easily accommodate a wide range of devices including hard drives, CD-ROMs, and scanners. It has taken years for other specifications including USB to begin to catch up. Table 7.1 lists the current members of the SCSI family.

To use a SCSI drive or other device in your system, you'll need three elements: a device of a particular standard, the appropriate cable from the device to the adapter, and the proper adapter. In general, SCSI adapters are downwardly compatible, meaning that, given the proper cable, an Ultra SCSI adapter will support fast, wide, and basic SCSI devices.

SCSI devices can be installed within the case of a PC as an internal unit, although they are more commonly external devices.

Your most important assignment in installing a SCSI drive is to obtain a cable with the proper connectors at each end.

The original SCSI specification required male DB50 50-pin connectors, the same as those used on serial and parallel devices, for the adapter. At the device, SCSI units expected a Centronics 50 male plug.

Table 7.1
Current Members of the SCSI Family

Common Name	Standard	Bus Width	Bus Speed	Maximum Transfer Rate
SCSI	SCSI	8 bits	5 MHz	5 MB/sec
Fast SCSI	SCSI-2	8 bits	10 MHz	10 MB/sec
Wide SCSI	SCSI-2	16 bits	5 MHz	10 MB/sec
Fast-Wide SCSI	SCSI-2	16 bits	10 MHz	20 MB/sec
Ultra SCSI	SCSI-3	8 bits	20 MHz	20 MB/sec
Ultra-Wide SCSI	SCSI-3	16 bits	20 MHz	40 MB/sec
Ultra2 SCSI	SCSI-3	8 bits	40 MHz	40 MB/sec
Ultra2-Wide SCSI	SCSI-3	16 bits	40 MHz	80 MB/sec
Ultra160 SCSI	SCSI-3	32/64 bits	40 MHz	160 MB/sec

SCSI-2 used a smaller Mini Centronics connector, also with 50 pins, for the device, and a variety of connectors at the adapter end.

SCSI-3 uses a Mini D68M connector, with 68 pins, for the device and controller.

If you're installing an internal device, you'll need a cable with a small card edge connector for the adapter and the appropriate connector for the device itself.

Unless you purchase a drive and controller in a package, you're almost certain to find a mismatch of cables and connectors. A good computer store or catalog will offer a wide range of cables and converters that adapt connectors as needed.

SCSI devices include a SCSI-in and SCSI-out port. The cable from the adapter or from the previous device on the chain goes to the incoming port. Additional devices on the chain connect to the outgoing port.

You'll also need to determine the termination needs of the devices in the SCSI chain. Think of a SCSI system as a pipeline under pressure; it needs to be capped, or terminated, at each end of the pipe to keep data from spilling out. The adapter itself is usually terminated, and you'll also need to terminate the last device on the SCSI chain. Termination can be accomplished by plugging a special dead-end plug on the SCSI-out connector; some devices allow you to turn on termination by flicking a switch or putting a jumper into place.

If you have a SCSI chain that extends in both directions from the adapter, you'll need to terminate the devices at each end. One example would be an adapter with a cable that goes to an internal device and another cable that connects through the back of the PC to an external SCSI chain. You'll need to terminate the internal device and the last device on the external cable; do not terminate the adapter in this instance.

A small number of motherboards come equipped with SCSI circuitry on the motherboard. This can be a good thing, because it should eliminate configuration issues; on the down side, the adapter may not be the most current implementation of the SCSI standard.

Installing a SCSI Adapter

One example of a basic and well-proven adapter is the Adaptec AHA-2930C, shown in Figure 7.5. This Ultra SCSI adapter is supplied with a number of external devices, in this case as the controller for an Imation CD-R. Adaptec provides an external port for the cable to the CD-R, which in turn also has an output for other devices on the SCSI chain. You can also attach a device to the internal SCSI connector on the Adaptec card.

You can install more than one SCSI adapter in your PC, and that is sometimes a good solution for unusual devices that come with matched adapters and drivers that are fine-tuned to work with a particular controller.

Another example of an all-purpose SCSI card is the AP-40, from SIIG.

Figure 7.5

An Adaptec Ultra SCSI adapter packaged with external devices.

Figure 7.6

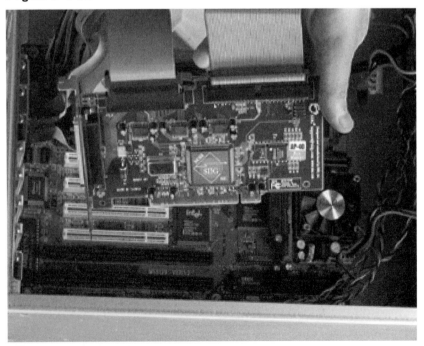

An all-purpose SCSI card for internal and external devices.

Figure 7.7

The adapter, shown in Figure 7.6, provides support for UltraWide, Ultra SCSI, and Fast SCSI devices. As a PCI device, it is configured under plug-and-play on a Windows system.

It provides an external high-density 68-pin connector, plus internal high-density 68-pin and 50-pin connectors. The system BIOS can be flash-updated with bug fixes or to provide new functions.

One way to customize your PC set-up is to build your own SCSI subsystem, like the one shown in Figure 7.7.

An external SCSI subsystem.

External SCSI cases are available to hold one or more devices. This case has two bays and its own power supply. Hard drives, CD-ROMs, CD-Rs, and DVD-ROMs install in bays within the case and are interconnected internally. A single data cable runs from your SCSI adapter to the back of the subsystem.

The internal arrangement of my SCSI subsystem is shown in Figure 7.8.

FireWire (IEEE-1394) Ports

The arrival of high-bandwidth devices like digital still and video cameras, high-speed scanners, and other devices has been met with yet another variation of the serial bus.

The IEEE-1394 protocol, dubbed FireWire by Apple, began at a zippy speed of 100 Mbps and has already been boosted in some implementations to 200 and 400 Mbps. At the device end, a number of manufacturers including Sony, Panasonic, and Canon have begun promoting FireWire connections from video cameras. A single FireWire port can connect as many as 63 devices to a host computer, and like USB devices they can be plugged in or removed while the computer is running.

Few motherboards come with FireWire ports, but there are several easy plug-and-play upgrades available. One, from Adaptec, brings together an Ultra Wide SCSI interface and FireWire on the same card.

SIIG's 1394 FireWire 3-port PCI card, shown in Figure 7.9, includes three hot-pluggable FireWire ports. The card also includes a basic DV editing application for use with digital video cameras.

Network Interface Card

When the first PCs were introduced just over two decades ago, they marked a major shift away from what was then the model for computing: one large mainframe that served dozens of dumb terminals, essentially video screens and keyboards. Each user had to share the resources of the mainframe: storage of data and programs, the attention of the central processor, and devices such as printers.

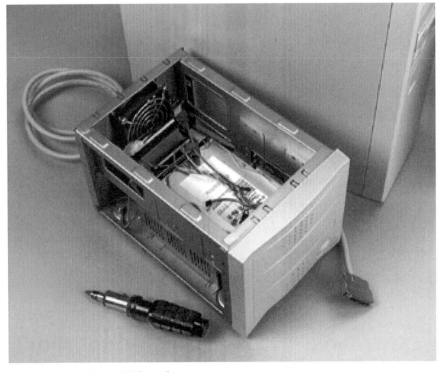

Figure 7.8

The interior of the SCSI subsystem.

Users of the first PCs reveled in the freedom to control their own destinies with a processor of their own, storage right at their desk, and access to printers and other devices without having to share them.

But as PCs became more and more common in offices, it began to dawn on users that there was a serious downside to this scheme. How could the CEO get information from accounting, inventory, and sales when each department or each worker was an independent island?

The solution was to connect the computers in a network. Each PC can still do its own work with its own resources, but users could share their data and devices with others easily.

Today, the network has even arrived in the home. Mom or dad can check on Willie or Tessa's homework; the kids can share an expensive printer or scanner.

Setting up a network requires three or four elements:

■ A network interface card (NIC) that provides a doorway to and from your system. The simplest and most common design establishes an Ethernet for your PCs.

■ A link between your computer and the others connected to the network. The link is usually a cable designed specifically for computer use, but it can also be a thin telephone wire or a wireless radio system.

Figure 7.9

A FireWire adapter card.

■ An operating system that includes networking protocols to manage the identification of machines on the network and the interchange of information among them.

■ For most network designs, a piece of hardware called a hub to bring together the various cables in a hub-and-spokes configuration. Some network "topologies" don't require a hub but rather directly connect one machine to the next one down the line.

For most home and small-business users, all current Ethernet NICs work very much the same way. The first choice buyers have to make is between a card that plugs into the ISA bus or one that connects through the PCI bus; if you can spare a PCI bus slot, that is the way to go. Not only is PCI faster and more capacious, but you should find that Windows' plug-and-play features work better with that connection.

I should also point out a pair of alternate means of adding a NIC to a current machine: one is an adapter that connects to the USB hub or port, and the second is a PC card that installs in a portable computer or, on rare occasions, in a PC with a PC card slot. The advantage of these cards is that they do not require internal installation and do not demand one of the system IRQs; they are somewhat more expensive than a card that plugs into the bus.

The second important choice involves the network speed. Current Ethernet cards are available in 10 and 100 MB per second (fast Ethernet) versions. Faster is better, although a bit more expensive.

To achieve fast Ethernet speed, all of the components of the network have to meet that specification: the NICs, the hubs, and the cable that interconnects them.

Do you need fast Ethernet? In a small home or business operation with half a dozen users, you're not likely to notice the difference. The additional speed is worthwhile if you expect to have a great deal of network traffic; in my office, with ten machines on the network, there is rarely a situation where more than two machines are talking to each other or communicating with a printer at one time.

The third choice involves the type of connector. The simplest type of wire is category 5 cable, a beefed-up version of a simple telephone cable that terminates in a plastic click-in connector called an RJ-45. These cables are easy to lay along the floor or within the wall and are inexpensive.

A pricier cable is coaxial, similar to the wiring used for cable television. Some building codes require the use of this heavier, fire-resistant media, although that requirement is changing in many locations. Coaxial cable uses a screw-in metal connector. It is more expensive and is heavier and more difficult to manage on the floor or wall.

Figure 7.10

Network interface card.

Phone Line Networks

A near-cousin of Ethernet systems are home phone line networks. These systems promise simple configuration and use of an interconnection that uses the existing telephone wires in a small office or home to carry data and share devices.

Early implementations of the concept yielded transfer speeds of about 1 MB per second; later versions claimed to match basic Ethernet speeds of 10 MB per second.

The systems require installation of a network adapter in a PCI bus or an external device that connects to a USB port. A telephone wire connects from the adapter to the phone outlet; the telephone can be used for ordinary communication even with a phone line network in use.

Installing a Network Interface Card

An example of a basic NIC for an ISA bus slot is shown in Figure 7.10.

At bottom left of the ISA NIC, shown in Figure 7.11, is an open socket for a BIOS chip that allows the network card to serve as a boot device. In this way, a PC becomes a workstation by deriving all of its operating system, applications, and data from a host machine. A pure workstation does not have a hard disk of its own.

The single connector on the bus bracket is for an RJ-45 plug of an Ethernet network.

A more advanced version of a NIC is shown in Figure 7.12. This card, which installs in a PCI bus slot, has no jumpers or switches to be set; all configuration is performed through a software menu. The plug-and-play device supports 10Base-T Ethernet and the newer 100-Base-TX Etherfast protocol.

You'll need a 100-Mbps hub or a dual-speed 10/100-MBps hub to work with an Etherfast NIC.

Figure 7.11

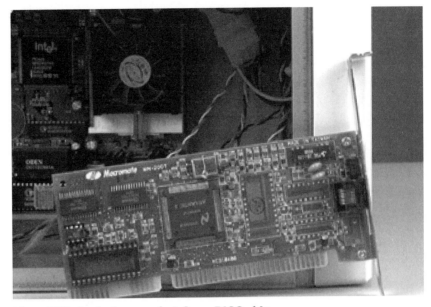

Many NICs include a socket for a BIOS chip.

Figure 7.12

A current NIC for the PCI bus.

CHAPTER 8

Sight and Sound

Project 5: Video Cards

Project 6: Sound Cards

The first computers had one basic purpose: they were very high-powered calculators that yielded an answer in the form of a number. The number could be reported on a dial, on a panel of flashing lights, or, eventually, in the form of a simple electrical signal that caused a teletype to tap out a printed answer.

In just the relatively short period of a few decades, we have reached a point where even the simplest of computers report their findings by drawing exquisite pictures and flows of words on a video screen or even by talking to us.

The very first IBM PC set the mode for all of the machines we use today. The computer itself had no way to communicate with the outside world; to convert its bits and bytes into something visible or audible, the data has to pass through an *adapter* that plugs into the bus.

Although that may seem like an extra step, in many ways it is a very good thing because it has led to a steady advance in the capabilities of personal computers over the years. Today, nearly every current PC can easily be upgraded or changed to add the latest and greatest displays and audio features or adapted to special purposes such as touch screens or text readers for the blind.

In this chapter I discuss removing an older graphics or sound card and replacing one or both with newer, more capable versions.

A Quick Course in Video Adapters

Every video adapter does the same thing. It takes in information from the computer's memory and then outputs it in a signal that can be displayed on a computer monitor.

It is on the card where the important differences lie: the resolution of the image it produces, the number of colors in the digital signal, and the speed with which it can construct an image from the information provided by the computer. I'll explain each of these components.

To understand *resolution*, you'll need to consider the way a computer monitor or television screen displays an image. What you see on the screen is made up of hundreds of thousands or millions of individual colored dots; up close that's all you would see, but at a proper viewing distance of a foot or two from the screen, the dots merge into a picture. Each of the dots is called a *pixel*, or picture element.

The more pixels per inch, the finer the resolution of the monitor. It's important to remember that the video adapter and the monitor are dependent on each other: a monitor cannot display more pixels than a video adapter is capable of including in a signal, and a video adapter cannot demand a monitor to work with more pixels than it is capable of displaying.

The basic PC resolution, called *VGA*, displays 640 pixels horizontally and 480 pixels vertically, for a total of about 300,000 dots. (The measure is inexact because the image usually extends a bit beyond the visible borders of the monitor's screen.)

The top end resolution for consumer-level adapter and monitor combinations is 1,600 by 1,280, yielding nearly seven times as many pixels on screen.

Pixels, by the way, are actually a triad of dots—red, green, and blue—that in combination are illuminated to produce colors.

When you're considering purchase of a *monitor*, it's important to look at one other measure: *dot pitch*. This tells you how closely together the dots are placed. The finer the dot pitch, the finer the image. In the case of pitch, smaller is better; look for a dot pitch of 0.28 mm or less. Monitors that use Triniton tubes use a slightly different measure, called *grille* or *slot pitch*; for these monitors, a measurement of 0.25 mm or less is good.

Another measure of monitor quality is *refresh rate*, a measure of how often the monitor rewrites the screen. The higher the refresh rate, the more stable the image appears. A slow refresh rate makes the image seem to flicker.

The television in your den is an analog device. *Colors* exist as a point on a continuous range that theoretically extends from zero to infinity; this allows for a great deal of subtlety in colors but also a great deal of inaccuracy from one TV to another or from one setting to another.

Computer monitors, in contrast are digital devices. Colors exist as precise numeric values within a predetermined set of colors. The original video adapters for the PC used a palette with as few as eight colors; resulting images were cartoonlike at best.

Today, current video adapters for consumer use can display colors from a 24-bit palette, also called *true color*. In computer terms, this works out to 16,777,216 colors. (Some cards offer 32-bit palettes, which may be overkill for most nontechnical uses.)

The more colors the adapter uses to build its signal, the more memory it requires. Therefore, higher resolution demands more memory.

Most video cards use specialized high-speed memory mounted directly on the adapter. Current cards usually offer a minimum of 8 MB of video RAM; high-end video cards for gamers and designers offer 32 or 64 MB and more. Some cards can be upgraded with additional memory after they have been purchased; consult the instruction manual for details.

(A handful of "bargain" PCs use built-in video adapters on the motherboard that share a piece of system memory for their purposes. Not only is such an arrangement slower than dedicated video RAM on an adapter, but it also puts a load on the microprocessor and reduces the amount of RAM available for the operating system and applications. If you find yourself with a PC that uses this sort of video circuitry, I would highly recommend upgrading your system with a new video adapter. Consult the PC's instruction manual for necessary steps to disable the onboard video adapter.)

The final element of a good video adapter is its speed in constructing images and sending them out the pipe to the monitor. Faster is better, and it's a pretty safe bet that any current video card is speedier than a model as little as a year old. You can check the specifications of video cards in search of ratings such as megapixels per second (millions of pixels per second) or bandwidth ratings.

You'll be hard-pressed to find a video adapter to plug into an outmoded ISA slot. Current adapters use the PCI bus or the even faster AGP (accelerated graphics port) connector on the most current of motherboards.

Determining Video Settings

To check on the current settings for your video adapter under Windows 95 or 98, click on Start/Settings/Control Panel/Display and go to the Settings tab. You'll see a report like the one shown in Figure 8.1.

You can get to the same report by right-clicking anywhere on the desktop and choosing Properties and then the Settings tab.

From the same page you can make changes to the number of colors or resolution, with your options limited by the capabilities of the video adapter currently installed.

Installing a New Video Card

If your PC has a video adapter in place, most upgrade projects begin with its removal. (I'll discuss two-adapter, two-monitor set ups later in this chapter.)

If your PC has video circuitry on the motherboard, consult the system motherboard to determine if you need to move a jumper or switch on the motherboard to disable it; on some systems, the BIOS can detect the presence of a new video card in the bus and disable the motherboard's circuitry automatically.

In Figure 8.2, I'm removing an older graphics card from the PCI bus of the demonstration machine.

The old ATI graphics card, shown in Figure 8.3, has few special features and only 2 MB of video RAM.

For this upgrade project, I'm installing a PowerColor video card, an off-brand adapter used by some system integrators. A close reading of the specifications for this non-name card reveals that it uses the 3Dfx Voodoo II graphics controller. 3Dfx also sells video adapters under its own name;

the company merged with STB Systems in 1999.

The PowerColor card, shown in Figure 8.4, includes 12 MB of video RAM and a full suite of three-dimensional features appropriate for high-end gaming and graphics. The card installs in the PCI bus as a replacement for the original video adapter. After installation, Windows 95 or 98 will direct you in configuring the proper drivers.

I also worked with another advanced video card, ATI's All-in-Wonder 128 card. This Swiss Army knife of a video adapter offers a bit of almost everything video, all in one place. The card is available in a PCI version and in a faster model for installation in an AGP slot.

The demonstration PC I've been using for upgrades to this point does not have an AGP slot. In the section that follows, I'll show how the AGP version of the card installs in another motherboard.

Figure 8.1

Display properties.

Figure 8.5 shows the ATI All-in-Wonder AGP card. The AGP connector is more toward the center of the adapter card than is a PCI connector.

In addition to high-performance three- and two-dimensional graphics based on the ATI RAGE 128GL Graphics Accelerator with 16 or 32 MB of video RAM, the All-in-Wonder card allows you watch television on your computer screen and capture images from TV, VCR, camcorder, or digital cameras. You can also output your computer images to a VCR or television set.

The television feature alone is among the more advanced consumer-level devices of its kind, including zoom-in, video capture,

Figure 8.2

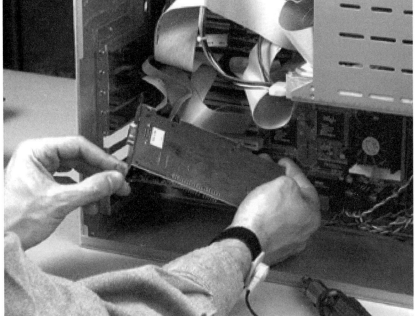

Removing a video card.

Figure 8.3

An older basic video card.

Figure 8.4

A modern video card.

closed captioning with "hot word" alerts, and a digital VCR with real-time video compression. The audio components of the card deliver dbx stereo sound where available.

The card offers a daunting combination of inputs and outputs. On the back panel is a monitor connector for a computer video display, an A/V out connector to send a computer image signal to a TV or VCR, a cable television connector, and an A/V input connector.

The A/V in connector is used to link to another four plugs on an external block; here you can receive an S-video signal for a VCR, camera, or DVD player; a composite video signal from a less sophistical video device; and left and right audio signals. The block merges all of these signals onto a single cable to connect to the adapter.

On the card itself are pin connectors to attach to CD audio, one of several ways to bring in sound for videos you create using the card.

The broad group of features on the card is managed by a suite of software. If you choose, the software will install a Launch Pad, as shown in Figure 8.6, on the desktop.

The buttons launch, from left to right, a DVD player, video CD player, video editor, television display, and CD audio.

The television set-up facility, shown in Figure 8.7, will automatically scan the incoming cable signal to preset all available channels.

Installing Two Video Cards and Monitors

Among the advanced features in Windows 98 is a facility to manage two display adapters and two monitors attached to the same system.

Why would you want two monitors on a single PC? The best example in my office is this: we run Adobe Photoshop for image editing and devote one large monitor and high-resolution video adapter to the display of the image. We use a second monitor solely for the display of the many menus and control panels of Photoshop. It's an elegant solution for this sort of intensive editing work; an example is shown in Figure

Figure 8.5

An AGP video card with multimedia features.

8.8. You could also use the two monitors to display different programs or to examine different files from the same word processor for side-by-side comparison. The two adapters can be set to the same or different resolutions and number of colors.

To install two display adapters, begin by installing and setting up one video adapter and monitor and making sure it is performing properly. Then install the second card in an available slot.

Depending on the BIOS and video adapter, some advanced multimedia or three-dimensional features may only be available on the card designated by the system as primary.

If you have a motherboard with an AGP slot, the standard configuration in most systems will make the PCI card the primary adapter and the AGP card the secondary; you may be able to override this somewhat illogical assignment from the BIOS screen.

In a system with two PCI video cards, the primary video card will usually be the one installed in the PCI slot with

Figure 8.6

TV Channels Initialization Wizard

This section helps you connect your TV to your cable or antenna.

Step 1
Select the proper cable or antenna for your region. USA Cable

Step 2
Press Autoscan. This searches through the range of channels for available channels. The process takes about 30 seconds. Autoscan

< Back   Next >   Cancel

A multimedia launch pad.

the lowest number. Slot numbers can be seen on the schematic diagram in the system instructional manual; on most motherboards, the lowest number PCI slot is the one farthest from the ISA slots.

Sound Cards

A sound card gives your computer a voice, an orchestra, and a set of ears. In years past there were several competing sound card specifications that were not compatible with each other. Today, nearly all sound cards include the features and commands of the Sound Blaster, the Windows Sound System, or both.

With a sound card, the PC can speak to you by playing back recorded digital speech or through a text-to-speech program. The PC can listen to you with voice recording and voice recognition features. A sound card can also play audio from a music CD or produce a wide range of sounds for business, education, and gaming applications.

The various types of sounds come to the sound card from different places.

The Windows operating system and applications that are installed on your hard drive use *.WAV (pronounced "wave") and similar digitized sound files that are interpreted by hardware components on the sound card. The data for these files travels to the sound card across the computer's system bus.

If you use Windows or an application to record your own voice, the files would be stored as digital *.WAV files. Most sound cards can also record music or sound from an outside

Figure 8.7

Television set-up for a multimedia video card.

Figure 8.8

Two video systems on one PC.

source such as a tape deck, video recorder, or the analog output of a CD player. The information for this source of information travels to the sound card as an analog audio signal that plugs into an input jack on the back of the sound card.

If you want to play the digital audio output of a CD-ROM player installed internally, you'll need to connect an audio cable inside the PC between the sound card and the digital output of the CD-ROM.

Figure 8.9

An older sound card.

Removing an Old Sound Card

If you need to remove an older sound card for an upgrade, a few moments of preparation will speed installation of a new card later.

Our demonstration machine was equipped with a Sound Blaster card, shown in Figure 8.9, an outdated ISA card with minimal memory.

As I disconnect the audio cable that connects to the CD-ROM I place a label on the connector; in most instances, the same cable can be used to attach to a new sound card. The cable is shown in Figure 8.10.

Figure 8.10

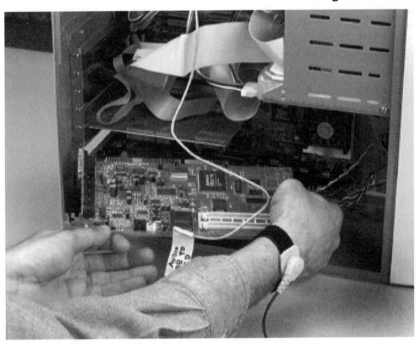

An audio cable from the CD-ROM to the sound card.

Installing a Sound Card

Installation of a sound card is straightforward; be sure you match the card to an available slot. Most current cards require a PCI slot; if you have a choice between a PCI or an ISA slot, use a faster and more capable PCI adapter. If you have an older machine or slots are in short supply, you should be able to find an ISA card, although these devices are limited to 16-bit processing and lack other advanced features.

The tricky part of sound card installation is allocating the proper IRQ and memory resources; an advanced card such as the Sound Blaster PCI512 requires one interrupt for 32-bit features and a second for Sound Blaster 16 emulation. On a current machine, use the facilities of plug-and-play to avoid conflicts.

Older ISA cards often employed jumpers or switches on the card for the assignment of IRQs and memory segments. You'll have to experiment with offerings in search of conflict-free settings.

The first of two sound cards I worked with for this project is a off-brand card from SIIG called the Soundwave Pro, shown in Figure 8.11. The card includes a connector for digital audio from older-style CD-ROMs and current devices, and four other connectors for TAD and internal and external Aux, Line, and Microphone.

Figure 8.11

A modern sound card.

Many audio cards, including this one, have a built-in power amplifier for use with unpowered speakers; to prevent an inadvertent burnout, the amplifier is usually turned off when the card is shipped from the factory. To turn on the card's amplifier, you'll need to change a jumper setting or throw a switch; consult the instruction manual for your sound card for details.

I then worked with a brand-name sound card with a wide variety of inputs and outputs, the Sound Blaster PCI512 from Creative Labs, shown in Figure 8.12. I purchased the card as a "white box" device from a discounter. The same product as you would find on the shelves of a computer retail shop, white box versions are sold without fancy packaging and "free" programs.

The PCI512 is an entry-level audio card, which is more than adequate for most home and business users, including support for high-quality three-dimensional gaming.

The card is based around Creative's EMU10K1 audio processor. Every signal is processed as 32-bit data, at 48 KHz, using eight-point interpolation to smooth the sound. In addition to signal processing for fidelity, the chip allows real-time addition of effects including reverb, chorus, echo, and pitch shifter.

The card will work with MIDI music devices that support the industry-standard MPU-401 UART or are specifically designed for use with Sound Blaster MIDI. The PCI512 also includes a gameport and a standard PC game control that will work with most analog joysticks; some more sophisticated joysticks may also require the MIDI adapter or a Y-cable to work with the card. Be sure to check with any joystick or MIDI device manufacturer for compatibility before you make a purchase.

Figure 8.12

A current entry-level Sound Blaster card.

On the card itself are three internal connectors:

■ A telephone answering device (TAD) for interconnection with some of the latest modems that include voice mail features.

■ A CD audio connector to link to the analog audio output of a CD-ROM or DVD-ROM drive, using a CD audio cable.

■ An AUX connector to link to internal audio sources such as a TV tuner, MPEG decoder, or other such device.

Current audio cards use color codes to mark the purposes of external connectors. Standard colors are:

■ Line in (blue). Connects to external, amplified devices such as a cassette player, reel-to-reel deck, or a stereo receiver.

■ Microphone in (red). Connects to an external microphone for voice input.

■ Line out (green). Connects to powered speakers or an external amplifier for audio output.

■ Rear out (black). Connects to powered speakers or an external amplifier for audio output.

Connecting a CD-ROM to the Sound Card

To direct the digital output of a CD-ROM to the inputs of a sound card, you'll need to connect the appropriate audio cable to both devices, as seen in Figure 8.13.

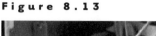

Most current CD-ROMs are packaged with an audio cable that matches standard sound cards. If the connectors do not match, you should be able to purchase the appropriate cable from a computer store or connect together two mismatching cables; the sound card or CD-ROM instruction manual should offer advice on how to do this.

The older CD-ROM I removed from the demonstration PC for the projects in this book came with a cable that did not match either of the two digital inputs on the new SIIG sound card, shown in Figure 8.14, above the pointer and above and to the right of the pointer.

The digital output of the CD-ROM meets the audio input on the sound card.

Redirecting Computer Sounds to the Audio Card

It is possible to redirect the sounds that normally come from your computer's speaker to the speakers connected to your audio card. Once you do this, however, you will not be able to hear POST beeps (computer beeps made during power-on self test).

To redirect your computer's sounds to external speakers,

1. Locate and remove the PC speaker connection from your motherboard,

2. Connect a wire from the +5V DC pin of the motherboard's speaker connector to pin 1 of your card's PC speaker connector, and

3. Connect another wire from the PC speaker-out pin of the motherboard's speaker connector to pin 2 of your card's PC speaker connector.

Advanced Software Features of a Sound Card

One of the advanced features of some sound cards is Environmental Audio, a system that processes signals to simulate a sonic environment.

Creative's implementation is an extension of Microsoft's DirectX and DirectSound 3D codes, shown in Figure 8.15.

You can instruct the sound card to modify sounds so that they sound as if they were being produced in environments ranging from a concert hall or arena to bizarre settings such as sewer pipes and closets.

Using the power behind the EMU10K1 audio processor in Sound Blaster PCI512, environments are constructed using X, Y, Z coordinates as well as reverberation and reflection cues to determine spatial information. These coordinates are used as the basic framework for channeling audio sources and effects to "paint" the audio scene. The audio environment really benefits from the use of more than two speakers, thereby widening the sweet spot to effectively create the most realistic experience.

The processing power needed to make the experience so intense and realistic requires the ability to route any audio source through multiple audio channels and add effects in real time. The EMU10K1, designed and developed at the joint Creative/E-mu Technology Center, can do this and much more. Using multiple speakers, the EMU10K1 accurately recreates and produces sounds as if they originated from different sources. It can also produce the acoustical features such as reverberation associated with a specific room, chamber, cave, tunnel, underwater channel, and so on.

At a minimum, support cues for distance, room size, and reverberation must be achieved for a "real" experi-

Figure 8.14

Internal audio cable connectors on a sound cable.

Figure 8.15

Environmental Audio control panel.

Figure 8.16

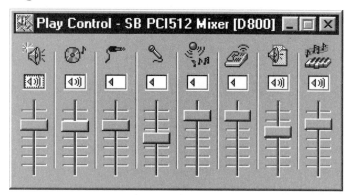

Audio mixer for a Sound Blaster card.

Figure 8.17

Multimedia control panel.

ence. The user needs more than just three-dimensional positional audio because the human ear does not just hear the origin of sounds. The ear also judges distance and resolves location and volume from many audio cues.

Most sound cards include a Windows-based audio mixer, like the Sound Blaster PCI512 mixer shown in Figure 8.16, that allows you to combine and manipulate sound from various audio sources. With Creative Mixer, it is possible to control the volume of an audio source while running other Windows applications. You can also select and mix different audio sources during play and recording.

A desktop control panel, like the one shown in Figure 8.17, controls various multimedia devices that work through the sound card.

Other advanced facilities, again from the Sound Blaster PCI512 suite, includes a panel to adjust the sound output to various speaker setups. In Figure 8.18, the card is adjusting for a room where the listener is seated in the middle of four speakers.

Multimedia Speakers

The only way I can recommend that you purchase a set of speakers is to make a visit to a computer store and listen to as many as possible to choose the one that sounds best to you.

You should consider purchasing a set of speakers that includes a powered subwoofer, which is enclosed in a large box that sits on the floor, out of the way. It is matched with small desktop speakers that carry the high-frequency sounds.

The combination works because low-frequency sounds are nondirectional. The heavy piece is out of the way but adds a great deal of presence to whatever you play through your sound card.

The desktop speakers of a three-piece system are shown in Figure 8.19; on the screen is a multimedia application to control the CD player.

Figure 8.18

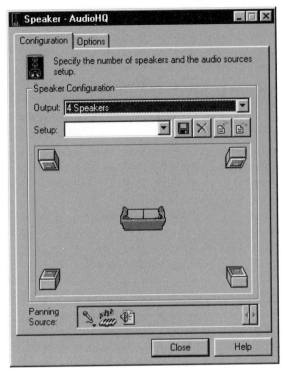

Audio sources set-up.

Figure 8.19

Multimedia speakers, with CD player and volume control applets on the screen.

CHAPTER 9

Brain Surgery

Project 7: Microprocessors and BIOS

Every other project in this book has dealt with the supporting actors of personal computing: the memory, storage, video, and sound. All of those projects served to expand and enhance the capabilities of PC, but they left untouched the engine that drives the entire system: the microprocessor.

The microprocessor is a wonder among wonders, a small block of silicon, metal, and plastic that is the brain of the computer. Even more wondrous is that, under certain circumstances, it is possible to give your PC a brain transplant.

Throughout this book I've written about how there are two separate but very important considerations before undertaking any upgrade project: Does the upgrade make technical sense? and Does it make economic sense? Nowhere do these questions have more importance than when it comes to brain transplants.

In this chapter, I discuss replacement CPUs that upgrade within a microprocessor family and conversion kits that promise to bring an outdated motherboard into the next generation. I also discuss a related upgrade project: installation of new a BIOS or reprogramming of a BIOS chip already in place.

About Microprocessors

The brain of the personal computer has evolved through seven generations, with nearly all of the branches coming from the Intel family tree. In recent years, however, a significant fraction of microprocessor sales has gone to other chipmakers, principally AMD.

The first IBM PC was based around the 8088 processor, a slow 8-bit device that today would be left way behind in the dust by your basic Game Boy.

Following generations included the 80286, 386, and 486 families. With the conditional exception of the 486 chip, all of the older microprocessors are now hopelessly outdated; motherboards and peripherals from these machines are not capable of running today's Windows operating system or working with current peripherals.

The modern era of processors began with the Pentium chip. That microprocessor was replaced by the Pentium II and later by the Pentium III, the last of Intel's 32-bit processors. The Pentium III uses a 32-bit internal architecture with a 64-bit data bus, like previous Pentium CPUs. Pentium III "B" series microprocessors support a 133-MHz system bus. Pentium III "E" series microprocessors include a number of advanced features; these chips use FC-PGA370 sockets that mount flat on the motherboard.

Intel's Celeron is a cousin of the Pentium II, introduced for economic reasons. It offers many of the features of the Pentium II at a lower cost; among the differences is a smaller block of cache memory. A Pentium III–based version of the Celeron is due by the end of 2000.

Over the years several companies have attempted to make a dent in Intel's dominant position as maker of microprocessors, including AMD, IBM, Cyrix, IDT, and Motorola. In the modern era, only AMD has managed to hold onto a small but still significant slice of the PC market. AMD's K5 chips were equivalents of Intel's Pentiums, the K6 chips were equal to or slightly better than Intel's Pentium IIs, and the Athlon processor a worthy competitor to Intel's Pentium III series.

Upgrade Options Within a Family

Most motherboards and associated BIOS and chipsets will work with a range of processor speeds within a particular family. For example, a current motherboard should work with Pentium III chips from 400 to 800 MHz in speed and certain compatible Celeron chips.

Consult the instruction manual for your motherboard and system for details of the type and range of speeds of microprocessors that can be used. In some designs you'll need to make changes to switches or jumpers on the motherboards. Most current designs will automatically detect and work with new compatible processors.

Once you know the acceptable range for your motherboard, you can consider purchasing a faster chip within the family of processors.

Intel has stopped making 486 and Pentium chips; you may be able to find supplies of chips in these families at some closeout sources. I'll discuss third-party conversion kits for these microprocessors shortly.

Intel has also all but ended distribution of Pentium II CPUs; as this book went to press, the only Intel Pentium II processor still officially supported by the company was a 450-MHz model, the last and fastest chip made for that series. You may find some orphaned Pentium II chips of other speeds from closeout sources.

As this book went to press, Intel was offering only a handful of Pentium III chips. The original chips in the series, which ran at 450-, 500-, or 533-MHz speeds, have been retired. Available chips for 100 MHz system buses began at 550 MHz and were extended to 700 MHz; a Pentium III running at 800 MHz for a 133-MHz system bus was also available.

In mid-2000, a typical price for the slowest Pentium III was about $299 and the fastest was about $799.

Technically, it is permissible to pull out a 450-MHz Pentium III and plug in a 700-MHz microprocessor. According to Intel's measurement of processor speed, the iComp 3.0 index, doing so would yield a theoretical processing boost of 1.6.

The question comes down to economics: Is it worth $800 to do so?

If you consider that you can purchase an entirely new computer, probably with a larger and faster hard drive, an even more advanced motherboard, and possibly a new suite of software for only a few hundred dollars more, you might decide that such an upgrade is not economically logical.

One strategy is to wait until the end of a product cycle and hope to obtain a faster microprocessor at firesale prices.

Upgrading Outside of a Family

If you own a computer based on an older Pentium II, Pentium, or late-model 486 microprocessor, you have a different set of options: in some instances, you will receive a reasonable benefit from installing a faster Intel, AMD, or Cyrix processor.

Weigh the costs of a replacement CPU against the claims of manufacturers and consider whether you might be better off saving the money toward the purchase of a new system. Remember that, no matter how fast the processor, you will be limited by the original design of the motherboard, including older memory designs and buses.

Earlier in this chapter I gave "conditional" approval to the continued use of a system based on a 486 chip. If you have a working computer based on that design, it may still have some value for a few specific assignments. For example, it can be used as a data entry workstation for simple word processing, spreadsheet, or database files. A 486 can run Windows 95—albeit after a painfully slow loading process—and can be placed on an Ethernet so that its files can be shared, and it can use printers and other peripherals on the network.

In my office, I keep alive a 486 66-MHz PC partly as a museum piece and partly as a training station for clerical help. It's perfectly acceptable for data entry; files created are sent across the network to a much speedier Pentium III for manipulation. I wouldn't begin to consider using it for photo retouching or audio editing.

Many systems based on 486 microprocessors can be upgraded one notch to Pentium equivalents by using upgrade chips that replace the original processor. Most of the upgrade chips use an adapted AMD K6-2 processor in a carrier that plugs directly into the socket formerly occupied by the 486. As this book went to press, such an upgrade sold for about $120.

You'll have to read the specifications for your old machine and the replacement chip very carefully. For example, the fine print on the AMD K6-2 upgrade just mentioned warns that, if your system's BIOS chips are especially old (about mid-1997 or before), this particular upgrade will not function properly.

I would not consider a CPU upgrade to a 486-based system unless the manufacturer of the upgrade promises compatibility with your specific set of socket, BIOS, chipset, and bus. That promise should be supported by a money-back guarantee if the new chip does not perform as promised, but I wouldn't pay more than about $120 for the privilege.

Upgrades for Pentium and Pentium II systems promise greater levels of compatibility, although I would apply the same criteria: look for a promise, in writing, that the upgrade will work on your particular system, with a money-back guarantee.

Pentium upgrades substitute Intel's original 75- to 166-MHz chip with an AMD upgrade that boosts processor speed to between 200 and 400 MHz. Pentium II models can be boosted with AMD or Intel Celeron replacement chips to speeds of as fast as 500 MHz.

However, remember that bus, memory, and peripherals will still lag well behind current systems.

With any upgraded microprocessor you might buy, make sure that the package includes a decent cooling fan; older systems may not have paid much attention to drawing away the heat generated by high-speed processors.

If it sounds as if I am lukewarm about microprocessor upgrades; that's because I am. The economics don't make a great deal of sense to me.

What Goes Where

Across the 486, Pentium, Pentium II, Pentium III, and AMD families of microprocessors included in this book, there have been 11 different designs for sockets or slots to hold the chips. Each of the receptacles includes a particular shape, number of pins, and electrical design.

Consult the instruction manual for your motherboard or system to be certain about the type of socket or slot in your PC.

Socket 1. 169 pins; 486 processors.

Socket 2. 238 pins; 486 processors.

Socket 3. 237 pins; 486, OverDrives, and early Pentiums.

Socket 4. 273 pins; early Pentiums.

Socket 5. 320 pins; Pentium 75 MHz through 133 MHz.

Socket 7. 321 pins; Pentium 75 MHz through 200 MHz, and Pentium clones including AMD K6-2 and AMD K6-III.

Socket 8. 387 pins; Pentium Pro, Pentium II OverDrives.

Slot 1 (SC242). 242 pins; Pentium II and Pentium III.

Slot 2 (SC330). 330 pins; Pentium II Xeon and Pentium III Xeon.

Socket 370 (FC-PGA370). 370 pins; Celeron to 533 MHz and Pentium III "E" series chips.

Slot A. 242 pins; AMD Athlon.

Pentium II, Pentium III, and Intel Celeron CPUs generally are mounted in upright holders that plug into slots in a manner similar to that of expansion cards in the system bus.

Figure 9.1

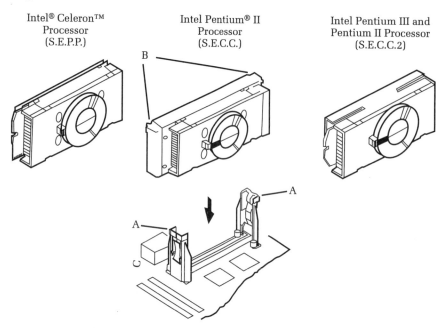

Intel® Celeron™ Processor (S.E.P.P.)

Intel Pentium® II Processor (S.E.C.C.)

Intel Pentium III and Pentium II Processor (S.E.C.C.2)

Intel Celeron, Pentium II, and Pentium III cartridges and installation.

The cartridges for each of the chips (and AMD's Athlon) are similar but not identical. Celerons use an S.E.P.P. cartridge. Older Intel Pentium II CPUs use an S.E.C.C. cartridge. Intel Pentium III CPUs and second-generation Intel Pentium II CPUs use an S.E.C.C. 2 cartridge. Figure 9.1 shows the installation of these cartridges.

Installing a CPU Upgrade to a Pentium or 486 CPU

The first step to installing a new microprocessor is the removal of the older CPU. As always, ground yourself before touching the interior of the PC.

In Figure 9.2, we see the Pentium 133 in its socket on the motherboard of our demonstration PC. The process of upgrading a 486 processor is very similar.

Figure 9.2

Intel Pentium in place on the demonstration PC.

The microprocessor is covered in this PC by a fan that attaches with clips at the top and bottom, as seen in Figure 9.3. Remove the fan carefully to expose the Pentium beneath.

On the motherboard of the demonstration PC, the fan drew voltage from a power source by a splitter that reduced a large connector to a smaller one, seen in Figure 9.4.

The zero-insertion force (ZIF) socket used for Pentiums and many other surface-mount processors locks the CPU in place with a clamping mechanism. Lift the handle, shown in Figure 9.5, to release pressure on the pins.

As you remove the Pentium, shown in Figure 9.6, note the notch in the upper left corner, which corresponds to the notched area on socket 7. You'll need to keep track of the notch for the reinstallation of a new processor.

Locate the notch on the replacement CPU. Figure 9.7 shows the underside of a PowerLeap upgrade. Check for bent pins. Carefully straighten them, if necessary; do not bend them back and forth or they will break.

Be sure the locking handle is up as you install the new microprocessor. The pins should mate easily with the openings in the socket; don't force pins. Once the microprocessor is in place, as seen in Figure 9.8, lower the handle and lock the upgrade in place.

Figure 9.3

Removing the microprocessor fan.

Attach the power lead for the fan on the new microprocessor to a power source from the power supply, as seen in Figure 9.9. Use a source that goes directly to the power supply, not to one that is shared with the hard drive or other device.

The final step on many microprocessor upgrades is to run a utility program supplied by the manufacturer; this will install any necessary drivers and may update the BIOS settings.

Figure 9.10 shows another upgrade product for a Pentium motherboard, a 366-MHz processor from Kingston Technologies.

Figure 9.4

Power connection for a microprocessor fan.

System BIOS Chips

The basic I/O system (BIOS) is the lowest-level set of instructions for your computer. One or more chips on the motherboard contain the instructions your hardware needs to bring itself to life when the power is first applied (called "booting" the computer, as in "pulling yourself up by your own bootstraps").The BIOS also stands between the microprocessor and the rest of the motherboard, informing the system about the bus design, I/O ports, video, keyboard, mouse, and other settings.

Figure 9.5

Zero-insertion force socket for surface-mount processors.

Older systems typically have one to four large BIOS chips installed in sockets on the motherboard. The chips were a form of read-only memory and could be upgraded only by removing them and replacing with newer versions.

More current systems generally have a single, larger capacity BIOS chip sometimes held in a socket and in other designs soldered in place. Most modern BIOS chips are electrically reprogrammable; you can obtain a new set of codes that can be read into the chips and stored there. The static memory design of the chips means that information is retained even when power is turned off.

Figure 9.6

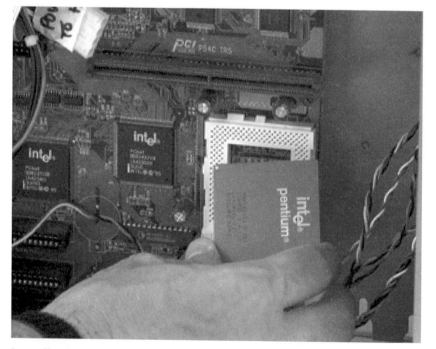

Installation notch on a Socket 7.

The BIOS works in concert with the system's chipset, a group of specialized controllers for functions including hard drive management, advanced buses, and memory.

Until 1994, PCs were unable to directly work with hard drives larger than 500 MB. It was a few years later before drives larger than 18 GB were recognized. These limitations were dealt with by changes to the BIOS in more modern systems.

If you have a very old system and need particular modern features not addressed in that BIOS, you may be able to purchase a replacement chip or an uploadable block of code. However, most users never have to replace or upgrade their BIOS; instead, it is often possible to use small bits of code called *drivers* to make changes to the basic operations of the computer. Every major hard drive maker now offers specialized installation programs and drivers to get around the roadblock on the size of hard drives.

Figure 9.7

Matching the notch on the replacement microprocessor.

Which BIOS Do You Have?

Most current motherboards use BIOS chips from one of three makers: Award, AMI (American Megatrends), or Phoenix. You may also find chips from lesser known Asian sources.

There are four ways to determine the manufacturer and version number for the BIOS in your system.

The best way is to pay attention when your system boots up; nearly every BIOS maker displays its name and a version number or date on the initial start-up screen. You may be able to make note of the infor-

Figure 9.8

Locking into place a replacement microprocessor.

Figure 9.9

Connecting a microprocessor fan to a power source.

mation as it flashes on your monitor. On some systems you can press the Pause key on the keyboard to freeze the start-up process. (Ironically, this is an element of only certain types of BIOS.)

Many utility programs, including System Information within Norton SystemWorks, can identify the maker of your BIOS and version, as shown in Figure 9.11. Some BIOS vendors also offer utility programs that will snoop within your system to display information about the chips used.

Another way to determine the maker and version of your BIOS is to remove the covers of the PC and locate the chipset, usually nearby the microprocessor on the motherboard. Most BIOS makers include their names and version numbers on a sticker on the chip or print that information directly onto the chip.

Figure 9.10

You may be able to learn about the BIOS from the motherboard or system information manual, although I have found this to be a somewhat undependable resource. Most motherboards will work with several different BIOS chips, and the instruction manual may not be up to date or may include information about more than one version.

Replacing or Upgrading BIOS Chips

Assuming your system is working properly, the best way to find out about available BIOS upgrades is to go on the Internet to vendors.

One source for the BIOS products of several companies is Unicore, reach-

Another microprocessor upgrade package.

able at www.unicore.com. You can also call the company at (800) 800-2467.

You can also go to the web pages of the manufacturers themselves, including Phoenix and Award (now merged into one company, but supporting both product lines.) Try www.award.com or www.phoenix.com. At these sites, you can find out about the capabilities of the latest BIOS products and link back to Unicore to place an order.

As I've noted, many current BIOS chips can be upgraded without being removed. You'll obtain or purchase a software program that will "flash" the reprogrammable chip with new instructions. Be sure to carefully follow the instructions from the BIOS maker to ensure that the new program is properly installed and verified.

Figure 9.11

Consulting the System Information report for BIOS information.

However you upgrade a BIOS, before you begin the process make a copy of all entries on your system's CMOS set-up screen to serve as a starting point for the new CMOS screen that will come with the updated BIOS.

Unicore will provide instructions on uploading new code to a reprogrammable BIOS or replacing older chips.

To remove a BIOS chip, turn off the machine and ground yourself before touching the interior of the PC. You may need to remove adapter cards or other components that may block access to the

Figure 9.12

Removing an old-style BIOS chip from its socket.

BIOS. Make notes and place labels on anything you remove to make it easier to replace them later.

Use a chip puller like the one shown in the section about tools and as shown in Figure 9-12; place the tool's hooks under each end of the chip and gently but firmly lift the chip out of its socket. To install a new BIOS, be sure to locate pin 1 on the socket and match it to pin 1 on the chip; carefully push the chip into place, taking care to see that all of the pins slide into corresponding holes in the socket. Watch out for any pins that might end up bent under or outside of the socket.

Eyes and Ears

Project 8: Scanners, Digital Cameras, and Headsets

To many in the computer industry, the future lies in computers that can see, hear, and speak. We've already looked at sound cards and video adapters, two essential elements of those capabilities. In this chapter, I discuss installation and use of external peripherals including scanners, digital cameras, a PC camera, and headsets.

A Short Course in Scanners

A scanner's job is to convert an analog drawing or photograph or a page of text into a digital file that can be manipulated by the computer.

The resulting image can be worked on in a digital darkroom program such as Adobe Photoshop or made an element of a web page or altered in a drawing program such as Adobe Illustrator. Run through an optical character recognition (OCR) program, a digital picture of a page of text can be converted into a file of characters to be edited in a word processing program.

A scanner works by shining a light on a target and then measuring the reflected brightness point by point and converting it into a computer bitmap. Color scanners measure the reflections from three separate lamps or light-emitting diodes (red, green, and blue) on the image or use a single light source that makes three passes through red, green, and blue filters.

A slide or transparency scanner works in a similar way. These devices, often used by graphics professionals or photographers, record a very fine resolution for the small area of a slide.

The quality of a scanner is related to its resolution and bit depth.

Resolution is a measurement of the fineness of the dots recorded by the scanner; think of this as the inverse of the way a monitor constructs an image from tiny pixels. The finer the dots, the higher the resolution. For screen displays, 72 or 96 dots per inch (dpi) is all that is necessary; if you're going to print out images you capture, you'll need a scanner that has a resolution of at least 300 dpi.

Bit depth tells you how many samples of color or tones of gray the scanner is capable of recording for each dot it discerns. The higher the bit depth, the more lifelike the representation of colors. Current scanners offer a minimum of 24 bits; more advanced scanners record at least 30 bits.

Understanding Scanner Specifications

When it comes to scanner specs, are more bits the merrier? Well, if you are buying a scanner to acquire black-and-white images, including text for OCR, all you need is one single bit. In line art, black is black and white is the absence of black.

The next step in scanning is color, which is made up of three channels (red, green, and blue) of information. Gray-scale scans use just a single channel. A 2-bit image has four shades of a single color: black, dark gray, light gray, and white. For every added bit, the number of colors or shades double. Table 10.1 shows the relation between bits and colors.

For most consumer-grade scanners, that's as high as the device will go for each of the three colors (red, green, and blue) scanned. A 24-bit scanner splits the image to three filtered sensors or, in older models, makes three separate scans; each scan contains bits of information.

Table 10.1
Relation Between Bits and Colors

Bits	The Math	Colors
1	1×2	2
2	2×2	4
3	$2 \times 2 \times 2$	8
4	$2 \times 2 \times 2 \times 2$	16
5	$2 \times 2 \times 2 \times 2 \times 2$	32
6	$2 \times 2 \times 2 \times 2 \times 2 \times 2$	64
7	$2 \times 2 \times 2 \times 2 \times 2 \times 2 \times 2$	128
8	$2 \times 2 \times 2 \times 2 \times 2 \times 2 \times 2 \times 2$	256

The resulting color screen image or file on disk is made up of red, green, and blue channels, each containing as many as 256 distinct colors or shades.

Here's the math for a 24-bit scanner:

8 bits $\times$ 3 colors = 24 bits

24 bits = $256 \times 256 \times 256$, or 16,777,216 possible colors.

You'll also find some 30- and 36-bit consumer-grade scanners; high-end professional drum scanning models are typically 42 bits (three channels of 14 bits each).

Working with a Slide Scanner

The Olympus Film Scanner ES-10, shown in Figure 10.1, is a consumer-level transparency scanner that sets up with ease and performs well. Priced well below professional models, it delivers a maximum scanning resolution of 1,770 dpi at 24 bits of depth. Models connect to the PC through the parallel port or a SCSI adapter. The scanner comes equipped for 35-mm film; an optional module will hold Advanced Photo System cartridges.

This basic model lacks some of the advanced features of much more expensive transparency scanners, but many users may decide the trade-off is worth the savings. You'll need to manually refocus the scanner with an onscreen contrast scale each time you change holders or film type, and you'll have to inform the system of the film stock you're using at each session.

Figure 10.1

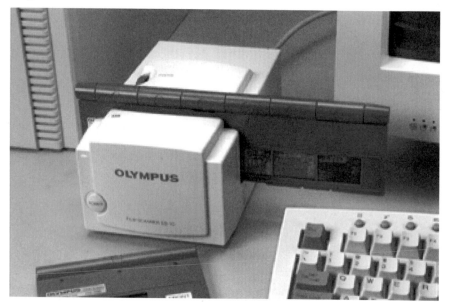

A desktop transparency scanner with negative carrier in place.

The parallel version of the scanner won't set any land speed records—a high-resolution scan takes 330 seconds—but set-up and use is as easy as that with any device you'll find. The resolution and image quality of this scanner is sufficient for most amateur and semiprofessional use, producing scans for use on web pages, for book-size publication, and at sizes up to 8 × 10 inches.

The ES-10 uses a TWAIN or TWAIN-32 interface, allowing scanning to be called from within many graphics applications, including Adobe Photoshop, and the simpler, supplied program from Olympus.

You'll get the best results from your image editing software if you begin with a high-quality scan. The ES-10 scanner software, shown in Figure 10.2, permits a great deal of adjustment before the image is captured.

A properly exposed and well-lighted image will likely work with automatic scanning exposure and color balance, but you can also make adjustments to the image based on a preview scan. In addition to sliders for exposure and color, you can display gamma and contrast curve controls that permit adjustment to individual red, green, and blue (RGB) channels of the image or all three elements of the RGB data at the same time.

Pen Scanners

For many years desktop scanners have provided a reliable, if somewhat inconvenient, way to transfer information from a printed page into text that can be manipulated and stored by the computer. The next generation in input devices includes hand-held scanners that allow you to swipe and scan lines of text from newspaper articles, books, and magazines.

One such product is the QuickLink Pen, from Wizcom Technologies, shown in Figure 10.3.

The device, a bit smaller than a television remote control and weighing just 3 ounces, includes a small scanner at one end, with tiny rollers to help you guide the pen along a line of type. At the end of each swipe, the device uses a built-in OCR chip to change the information to text that is then displayed on a small LCD.

The tiny device includes 4 MB of flash memory to store as much as 1,000 pages of data. The files can be transferred as you scan or when convenient by using an included serial cable or over a wireless infrared link to a PC or laptop that can work with IrDA devices. Output can also go to some other handheld devices including Palm Pilot and Windows CD units.

Figure 10.2

Olympus ES-10 image capture from within Adobe Photoshop.

Quicklink's software can also scan business cards directly into Microsoft Outlook, insert e-mail addresses into an address book, and collect Internet URLs for transfer to your browser's bookmark or favorites file.

I found the device to be easy to set up and use, although the accuracy of the scans varied greatly, depending on the size and quality of the type you are scanning and your own skill at using the device. Nevertheless, it represents an interesting extension of the PC to the nondigital world.

Digital Cameras

If you had any doubt about the way that traditional camera makers see the future, consider the names of some of the biggest makers of digital cameras: Kodak, Polaroid, Nikon, and Olympus.

Digital cameras are still tools for photography with many of the most advanced facilities including autofocus, automatic exposure, and built-in flash. All that is missing is the film. Of course, therein lies the biggest difference: the resulting image is not captured as an analog exposure on light-sensitive film but rather as a bitmap of digital 0s and 1s that can be directly loaded into a computer.

Figure 10.3

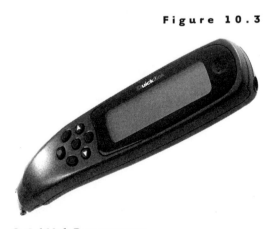

QuickLink Pen scanner.

Images are stored on magnetic media, including the matchbook-sized SmartMedia and the similar CompactFlash cards. One group of cameras offered by Sony stores images on standard 1.44-MB floppy disks. The media can be removed from the camera and loaded directly into a PC by using special desktop readers or downloaded over a serial or USB cable.

Digital images can be used directly on web pages and in presentations and can be printed with a photo printer.

The most objective measure of the quality of a digital camera is the number of pixels it can capture in each image. The more pixels there are, the more information is stored in the file, which permits bigger enlargements and better prints.

Figure 10.4

Olympus Camedia C-2020 digital camera.

Over the past few years, the number of pixels has doubled several times. Today, the basic snapshot digital camera captures images at 640 by 480 pixels, or about 300,000 dots. The high end of consumer-level digital cameras zoomed past 1 megapixel and then 2 megapixels in 1999; in mid-2000, owners of 3-megapixel cameras were looking over their shoulders at approaching 4-megapixel devices. As with many other parts of the computer industry, prices have stayed level or declined slightly even as capabilities have improved.

Also of importance is the quality of the autofocus and autoexposure systems of the camera; this is a subjective decision. Read the reviews of new cameras in enthusiast magazines and don't hesitate to visit a computer or camera store and spend some time trying out candidates.

Among the more advanced digital cameras are the members of the Olympus Camedia line.

I worked with the Olympus C-2020, a 2.1 megapixel camera with a 3X optical zoom and wide range of special features, shown in Figure 10.4.

Figure 10.5 shows, the Olympus camera connected by serial cable to the PC. The supplied Olympus software, shown in closeup in Figure 10.6, shows large thumbnails of six images taken in the photo studio.

The camera includes a color LCD on its back for previews of images; you can choose to erase any picture you don't want to keep. In Figure 10.7, six thumbnail images from the photo studio session are displayed.

The Olympus camera uses tiny SmartMedia digital film, shown in Figure 10.8, a form of static memory that does not require power to hold on to its contents. The supplied SmartMedia card holds 8 MB, large enough for about 16 photos at the camera's highest resolution using JPEG compression; an uncompressed TIFF file at highest resolution will take up the entire 8-MB card.

As this book went to press, SmartMedia cards as large as 64 MB were available. CompactFlash cards used in other digital cameras were available in sizes up to 192 MB.

Figure 10.5

A serial cable connects the camera to the PC.

PC Cameras

Figure 10.6

A PC camera is a direct input from your desktop into your computer. Uses include video telephone calls and web snapshots.

One example is the Intel PC Camera Pro Pack, which adds some advanced video functions to a USB-equipped computer. The mushroom-shaped module, which sits on the desk or on top of the monitor, can take still-frame snapshots at 640 × 480 resolution or full-motion video; either can be stored on disk or sent over the Internet for video phone calls or video e-mail.

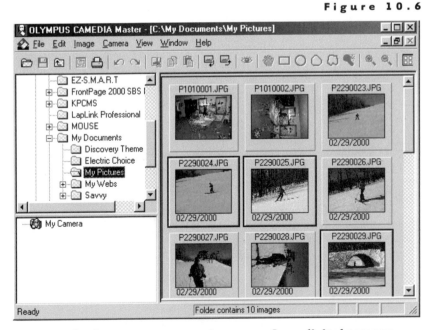

A companion image management program for a digital camera.

Figure 10.7

LCD display on the back of a digital camera.

A video input plug on the device also allows you to attach a VCR, camcorder, DVD-D, or other source of video images. Your computer can then play, record, or edit video images for posting on a web page or transmission over the Internet.

The package also includes Intel Video Phone software that permits video phone calls over dial-up and broadband Internet connections.

The Intel PC Camera Pack offers the same camera and video phone features, but does not include the video capture circuitry of the Pro version.

Headphones and Headsets

Some of the more interesting applications for the home and office use speech recognition and speech recording. You can dictate to your machine, give verbal instruction commands, and interact with databases and amazing games. Computers can also be used as a high-tech (and inexpensive) telephone over the Internet.

These amazing software applications and audio hardware require the use of a microphone for sound input; unfortunately, many of the microphones and headsets included with these products are very inexpensive and of shoddy quality, more like the throwaway headsets for airline movies than a serious professional tool.

Figure 10.8

A matchbook-size SmartMedia memory card with 8 MB of storage.

If you're planning to make serious use of speech recognition or speech input, I'd recommend purchasing a quality headset that is specifically designed for your type of use.

A basic headphone and microphone, part of the IBM ViaVoice voice recognition program, is shown in Figure 10.9. One connector goes to sound card output for the headphones and the other connector goes to microphone input on the sound card.

A more advanced line of products for use with a wide range of software is offered by Plantronics, which was one of the original makers of light-weight communication headsets. One of their devices went to the moon with Neil Armstrong in 1969.

Figure 10.9

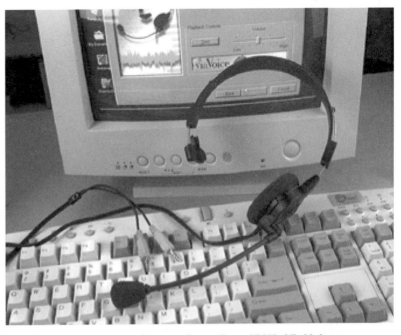

A basic headphone and microphone from IBM's ViaVoice program.

Among the features of a professional device are optimization of the sound output of the microphone for speech recognition, canceling out background noise, and tuning of frequency response for the human voice.

The Plantronics HS1 headset, shown in Figure 10.10, is aimed at multimedia gamers. In addition to a stereo microphone that works well with speech recognition, it includes high-fidelity stereo speakers and dynamic bass response. Inline controls adjust the volume of the headset speakers and the microphone.

The Plantronics LS1 stereo headset, shown in Figure 10.11, emphasizes light weight for long-wearing comfort for games and speech recognition.

Specifically designed for speech recognition, the Plantronics SR1 headset, shown in Figure 10.12, is a monaural device, with a noise-canceling microphone that delivers a signal tuned to the human voice and office environments.

Figure 10.10

Plantronics HS1 Hi-fi stereo headset for multimedia games.

Reaching into the Monitor with a Graphics Tablet

Your basic computer mouse is a wondrous device, allowing you to reach into the screen and move items with ease. A graphics tablet takes the concept a step further by offering a specialized pen that transfers a drawing from a pad into painting and word processing programs and a programmable mouse.

Figure 10.11

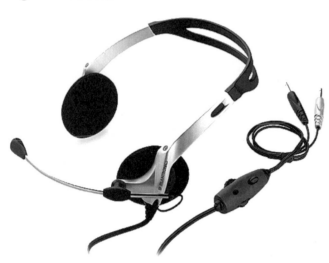

Plantronics LS1 light-weight stereo headset.

Figure 10.12

Plantronics SR1 Monaural speech recognition headset.

One example is the Wacom Graphire Tablet, which includes a wireless, batteryless pen and mouse. The Graphire pad draws a small amount of power from the computer's mouse or keyboard port and its serial port and detects changes in an electrical field made by the pen or mouse.

Wacom's resonance technology sends a tiny amount of power to a grid of wires in the pad, alternating between transmit and receive modes about every 20 microseconds. The mini broadcast antenna stimulates a coil in the pen or mouse that resonates a signal back to the grid.

The pad is capable of detecting 512 levels of pressure from the pen, allowing an artist to adjust shades and use tools very much like a pen on paper. An "eraser" on the top of the pen works just like the real thing.

The PenOffice SE software lets you add handwritten notes and comments to Word 97/2000 documents and saves them in Word format. I have used the device to "sign" documents on screen for printout or transmission as an e-mail attachment.

The Graphire product is available in versions that connect to the serial or the USB port; a second connector attaches to the keyboard or mouse port to draw power. You can continue using an existing keyboard or mouse with the Wacom product.

Universal Serial Bus

Project 9: USB Port and Devices

The USB has finally arrived for Windows machines, delivering users to the promised land of an almost unlimited chain of desktop peripherals.

I've already discussed the USB technology in the section on I/O ports in Chapter 7. Remember that you'll need to run Windows 98 to obtain all of the benefits of the USB.

In this chapter, I discuss how to add USB ports to a system born before the bus pulled into town, and then explore some of the more interesting devices that plug into the port.

Adding USB Ports

Most motherboards manufactured in 1999 and later include two USB ports. If you have a PCI bus motherboard, it is a simple matter to install an expansion card that adds two ports.

Figure 11.1

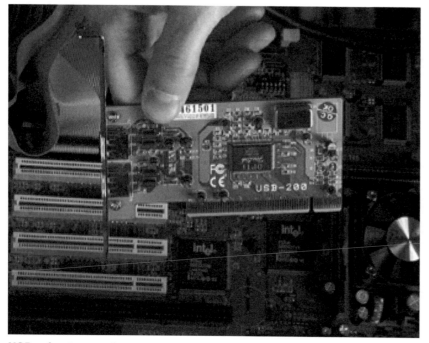

USB adapter card.

One example is SIIG's USB DualPort PCI, a plug-and-play adapter that requires no settings on the card or the system. Windows 98 will automatically detect its presence and direct you in installing the standard PCI USB driver.

The card, shown in Figure 11.1, can also be used to add more ports to a motherboard with the standard set of two USB ports. If you use the card as a second set of hubs, you are adding to the electrical draw on your power supply, because most USB devices take their power from the USB cable.

The USB adapter will be automatically detected by Windows 98. The two ports on the back of the adapter can work directly with individual devices or can be connected to one or two hubs to expand connection options and to add more power to the circuit.

Figure 11.2

The demonstration PC with its new USB chain.

As shown Figure 11.2, our demonstration PC is now equipped with a pair of USB ports added by an internal adapter card. A four-port USB hub is attached to one of the ports on the rear of the machine; connected to the hub is a USB keyboard, mouse, and modem.

Figure 11.3 shows the USB hub unplugged. Depending on the power demands of the devices, you may need to provide a boost to the available amperage on the hub. Of the three devices attached here, the modem is likely to demand the most power.

There are few limits on the types of devices that can be attached to a system through a USB port.

Devices already on the market include printers, scanners, keyboards, mice, modems, and Ethernet adapters. There have also been storage devices including Zip, SuperDisk, and Orb drives and a small number of external hard disk drives. With the arrival of USB 2.0, the protocol will likely embrace all manner of storage devices including hard drives, CD-ROMs, and backup devices.

USB Keyboard

The USB NetStation 3000X keyboard from SIIG, shown in Figure 11.4, offers all of the regular Windows keys as well as a Windows control panel and application keys, 20 hotkeys (10 of which are user programmable), direct operation with Internet browsing, and multimedia audio CD, video CD, and DVD playback. Installation requires three separate hardware wizard sessions under Windows 98 to add components.

Figure 11.3

There are three sets of special keys arrayed across the top of the USB keyboard.

The cluster at the upper left of the board, shown in Figure 11.5, offer specialized system controls. From left to right, the keys are:

Hotkey. Displays a user-configurable menu of special functions.

Z. Puts the system into Suspend/ Sleep mode, available on current machines.

USB hub.

Cup of coffee. Places the system in Screen Saver mode.

Calculator. Displays the Windows calculator.

Paste. Pastes saved copy into an application.

At the top center of the keyboard, shown in Figure 11.6, are volume controls to raise, mute, or lower the master sound output for the system.

Ten buttons at top right on the keyboard, shown in Figure 11.7, offer expanded Internet and audio and video player controls.

Figure 11.4

An advanced USB keyboard.

From left to right, the upper buttons are:

WWW. Launches the default browser when you are connected to an ISP.

BACK. Returns to the last page viewed in your browser.

SRCH. Launches the default search engine for your browser.

STOP. Halts the loading of a web page.

NEXT. Goes forward to the next page on an Internet browser

SCROLL. Scrolls up or down on the page; this key is optimized to work with Microsoft's Internet Explorer or Netscape Navigator.

The lower set of buttons controls the computer's CD or video players:

Figure 11.5

System controls.

Rewind. Returns to the beginning of the current track or to the previous track if no files are playing.

Play/Pause. Begins playing or pauses music.

Stop. Stops playing the current track.

Forward. Advances to the beginning of the next track.

Record. Records from an assigned source, such as a CD.

USB Mouse

The Logitech USB Wheel Mouse, shown in Figure 11.8, adds a scroll wheel between the two buttons. Turn the wheel to move up and down on your screen in most Windows applications and on the Web.

You can have more than one mouse on a USB chain, allowing quick and easy changes from one design to another or from one user to another. Logitech's device also comes with an adapter, permitting it to be connected to a PS/2 serial port.

USB Modems and Network Interfaces

The tiny USB data and fax modem, shown in Figure 11.9, draws its power from the port or hub. It is capable of connecting at speeds of up to 56 K.

I also worked with an elegantly simple USB Ethernet adapter from Shark Multimedia. This plug-and-play gadget, not much bigger than a cigarette lighter, brings all of the functionality of a 10Base-T network interface card without the need to open the PC case. There's also little chance of an IRQ conflict, something that is fairly common with internal NICs.

As with other USB devices, the Ethernet adapter is hot-swappable. Shark also offers pocket USB modems, DSL modems, and home networking devices including the Pocket USB Home LAN that includes a 56 K modem and a 10-Mbps networking connection that uses existing copper telephone wires in the home.

Figure 11.6

Volume controls.

USB Camera

SIIG's simple screen camera, shown in Figure 11.10, allows video conferencing and quick Web image capture.

USB Converter

An interesting bridge across technologies is a USB-to-parallel cable, like the one shown in Figure 11.11. The adapter takes in data over a USB link at the computer or hub and outputs bidirectional parallel signals at the other end. Windows printer drivers believe they are communicating with

Figure 11.7

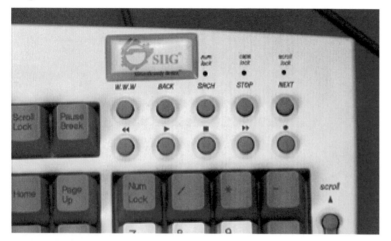

Internet and multimedia controls.

a USB device; printers believe they are working with a standard parallel port.

This adapter, which draws its power from the bus, allows you to hold on to your older parallel printers for use on a machine that might not support parallel devices directly. This also allows you to concentrate all of your output on the USB bus for convenience.

Figure 11.8

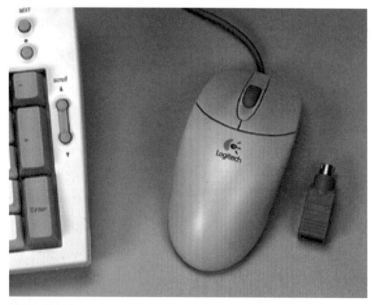

USB wheel mouse.

Figure 11.9

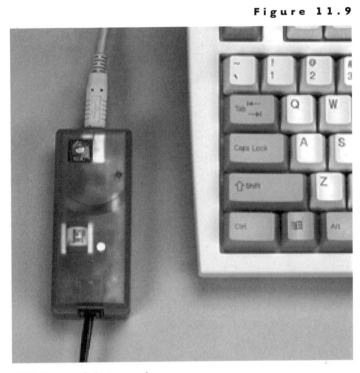

USB fax and data modem.

Figure 11.10

Screen camera with a USB connection.

Figure 11.11

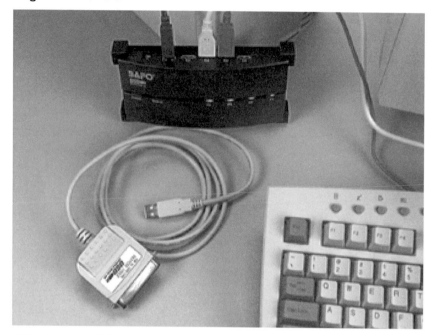

USB-to-parallel converter.

CHAPTER 12

A Place to Hold Your Stuff

Project 10: Motherboards, Cases, and Fans

Some cases perform their function in more style, and others are more convenient than others. If you're buying a new system or upgrading the case, there are three significant decisions to be made concerning type and size of the case, capacity of the power supply, and cooling and protection against RFV radiation.

Type and Size of the Case

A simple "pizza box" case takes up very little space on your desktop or can easily be hidden behind the desk or on the floor. Its disadvantage is its severe limitations on internal expansion room. You may not be able to install expansion cards or additional hard drives, CD-ROMs, or removable storage devices within the case. The power supply in small cases also is usually relatively weak, sometimes providing as little as 125 watts. With the spreading use of USB ports, however, most of these issues can be addressed with external devices, although going outside the box removes the advantages of its small size.

A large "tower" case offers abundant space for adapter cards and can hold as many as ten hard drives, CD-ROMs, removable storage devices, and other peripherals. Towers usually back up their capacity with full-size power supplies, often with as much as 250 watts of power. Towers can be placed on the floor or behind a desk.

An in-between solution that works for many users is a "mid-tower" that typically offers five to seven internal bays for devices and a hefty power supply of about 235 watts. Mid-towers take up the same amount of floor space as a full tower but are not as tall.

Upgrading from an older or smaller case to a modern unit is an exercise in physics, not in technology. Begin by matching the "form" of the motherboard; this determines the location of mounting holes and front and back cutouts for connectors and drives. Modern boards require an ATX case, whereas older boards are designed to be installed in an AT or AT compact case.

Capacity of the Power Supply

There are more and more sophisticated devices you can install within the case of your PC, including a wide range of storage devices. High-speed CPUs also draw more power than their older counterparts. Although designers have done a good job of reducing power requirements, the cumulative total demands of the motherboard and CPU, adapter cards in the bus, one or more hard drives, a floppy disk drive, a CD-ROM, and one or more removable drives can easily use up all of the power in the system.

The computer's power supply is a transformer that converts AC current from a standard electrical outlet into low-voltage DC current to run the computer. The power supply is mounted in a large metal box, usually at the rear of a desktop case or the upper rear of a tower case. A thicket of black, red, yellow, and white wires and connectors spread from the power supply to the motherboard and internal devices. Nearly all power supplies have a cooling fan that pulls air directly out of the case.

Luckily, motor-driven devices such as drives are not always running at full speed. Most draw the greatest amount of power when they are starting up from a dead stop, and many have energy-saving settings for when they are not in use. The biggest advantage would be in reading data from a CD-ROM drive for recording on a hard drive.

Cooling and Protection Against RF Radiation

The pulsing cycles of a CPU act like a miniature radio transmitter within your PC. Current medical research seems to indicate that this relatively weak RF radiation is not dangerous to humans, but that doesn't mean you should willingly add more signals from a box that usually sits very close to your body. However, the Federal Communications Commission (FCC) is concerned about interference with televisions, cell phones, garage door openers, and hundreds of other radio devices in our homes and offices.

All PC makers must certify to the FCC that their machines do not leak RF radiation, which is the reason cases are mostly made of metal, with additional metallic shielding within. (A handful of desktop cases and most laptop computers are made of plastic, with metal liners and special RF-absorbing materials within.) When the PC is delivered, slots on the back of the machine are sealed with metal closures. Even openings for air intake and fan outlet are often blocked with baffles to reduce RF leakage.

All of those internal devices, plus the power supply and a high-megahertz CPU, are sealed into a closed metal case. Think of an oven and you've got the right idea.

Therefore, it's very important that a PC case have adequate cooling. This can be accomplished in several ways, but the most common method uses one or more baffled openings at the front of the case and one or more fans at the rear to draw air across the innards. Nearly all current CPUs also have their own tiny fans or cooling devices mounted directly on the chip.

Except for an occasional short-term test, you shouldn't operate your PC with its cover removed or with open drive bays or uncovered adapter bracket openings. In addition to broadcasting RF signals, the openings will disrupt the channeled flow of cooling air over the sources of heat in the case.

You can also install additional cooling fans to an existing case. Various designs mount in drive bays, adapter brackets, and within the case itself.

(If you have the choice, spend a few dollars more for fans that promise quieter operation.)

Motherboard Form Factors

Motherboards do not exist in a vacuum. Just as they must be compatible with microprocessor sockets, industry standard buses, and connectors, they must also fit within a wide variety of cases. The connectors on the motherboard also must align properly with openings in those cases.

The solution has been a series of industry agreements on what are called *form factors.* As a result, computer manufacturers and upgraders can mix and match from among hundreds of combinations of cases and motherboards.

The most common form factors for current machines are ATX and AT in full-size and mini versions.

Today's most common and flexible design is the ATX, which will fit in ATX cases. These motherboards include a stacked I/O connector panel with serial, parallel, keyboard, mouse, and USB connectors. The CPU is in a central location so that an upright Pentium II or Pentium III can be installed without interfering with adapter cards.

A smaller version of current design is the Micro ATX, which has the same I/O layout as an ATX, permitting it to be installed in an ATX or Micro ATX case. Note, too, that ATX motherboards use a different design for their power supplies and require different electrical connections.

The full-size AT motherboard dates back to the design of the original IBM PC-AT. Serial and parallel ports and connectors for video output and the keyboard are located on adapter cards that plug into the bus. AT motherboards will only fit in AT cases.

The Baby AT includes some connectors directly on the motherboard; this design of motherboard will fit in AT and baby AT cases.

New Motherboards for an Older Machine

Changing the motherboard on an older machine is a major upgrade project. Doing so will involve every part of the machine: the case, the power supply, every drive attached to the computer, every adapter and stick of memory plugged into the motherboard, and everything that plugs into the computer.

This is not a project for the faint of heart or for those who insist on every project making economic sense. With the exception of a project to repair an otherwise worthy machine by removing a malfunctioning motherboard and installing an identical or near-identical replacement, you are almost certain to run into additional expense and all sorts of compatibility problems.

For example, if you upgrade an older motherboard with an ISA bus and SIMM sockets, you're likely to install a board with incompatible PCI slots and DIMM sockets. Your old memory will not fit, and most or all of your adapters cards cannot be carried over. The older microprocessor may not match the CPU socket or slot on the new board.

The best way to conduct a motherboard upgrade is to stop thinking of it as an upgrade but rather as a build-your-own PC project. The final cost will be equal to or greater than the price for a packaged system, but you will have a fully customized machine and the feeling of accomplishment that comes with the name you can stick on the front: yours.

A Sampler of Motherboards

An example of a current ATX motherboard is the Abit BE6-II, shown in Figure 12.1. Based around Intel's 440BX chipset, the board supports Intel Pentium III microprocessors from 450 to 700 MHz, Pentium IIs from 233 to 450 MHz, and Intel Celerons from 266 to 533 MHz.

The board includes an AGP slot for high-speed video, five PCI slots, and one ISA slot. Three 168-pin DIMM sockets support as much as 768 MB of SDRAM, with a 100-MHz external clock speed for the bus. Figure 12.2 shows a BE6-II motherboard before installation of components.

I/O facilities include an Ultra DMA/66 interface for four ATA/66 hard drives and other devices; a second controller manages as many as four ATA/33 drives. Built into the board are two USB connectors, a pair of serial ports, and a bidirectional parallel port. Other bells and whistles include built-in thermal sensors to monitor heat within the case,

Figure 12.1

Abit BE6-II motherboard in front of its new home.

Figure 12.2

The Abit BE6-II motherboard before components are installed.

Figure 12.3

Microstar MS-6182.

Figure 12.4

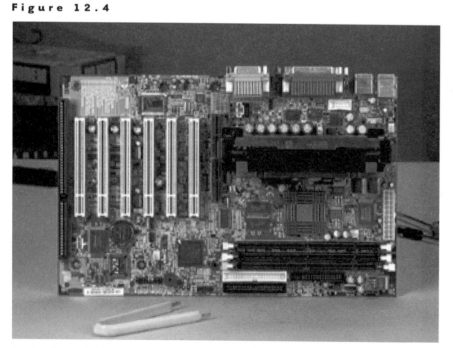

A Pentium III microprocessor stands in its vertical socket on the Microstar MS-6182 motherboard.

hardware monitoring of fan speed, voltages, and CPU temperature, connectors for infrared I/O, and advanced wake-on-ring and wake-on-LAN facilities.

The Microstar MS-6182 motherboard, shown in Figure 12.3, is a high-end slot 1 mainboard for Pentium II and Pentium III microprocessors, with an ATX form factor.

It is based on Intel's 810 chipset, which permits a highly integrated design that includes built-in three-dimensional graphics, support for Ultra ATA/66 hard drives, USB ports, and other advanced features. A video adapter is built into the motherboard, shown in closeup in Figure 12.4, with a connection equivalent to an AGP port.

This design of motherboard also has a connector for an Audio Modem Riser and PTI (PanelLink TV-out interface). These features are not yet in common use but are intended to permit direct plug-and-play installation of specialized devices for telecommunications and video input and output, with a more direct link to memory and the processor than they would have plugged into a PCI slot on the bus. On this Microstar motherboard, the AMR and PTI slots replace the AGP slot; the built-in video circuitry is mounted directly on the motherboard. The board is also available with built-in audio circuitry based on a Creative Labs design.

Figure 12.5

The Asus P5S-B Super 7 motherboard, a Baby AT, is a direct replacement for an older Socket 370 system, like the demonstration machine we've been upgrading. It is shown in Figure 12.5, with the Kingston Turbochip 366 in place, making the CPU roughly equivalent to a Pentium II 4,000 MHz.

This ASUS motherboard, shown in closeup in Figure 12.6, uses older CPUs of the original Pentium class and competitors from AMD, IBM, and Cyrix. On that older base, it adds support for modern features including PC100 memory, Ultra DMA/66 IDE hard drives, USB, and infrared interfaces. Versions of the motherboard also include built-in sound circuitry. Supported processors

Asus P5S-B Super 7 motherboard.

include AMD K6-2/266 and faster, AMD K6/166 and faster, AMD K5/100-133, IBM/Cyrix 6x86MX/M UU, and Intel Pentium 100–233 MHz chips. The board includes a built-in 2D/3D VGA video controller on the motherboard, using AGP circuitry for a speedy connection to the processor.

Adding Cooling to a Case

An 800-MHz Pentium III can get hot enough to fry an egg; more to the point, it can get hot enough to corrupt data, damage other components within the case, and eventually fry itself. This is the reason all current microprocessors include fans to draw heat away from them.

The next step is make sure that this heated air is properly drawn from the case. Begin by making sure that air intakes and exhausts are not blocked.

You can add an extra case fan, like the one shown in Figure 12.7, at the front of the case to help draw air through. Most modern cases have brackets and an opening for an additional fan.

Another, very simple way to add cooling is to install a slot fan such as the SIIG model shown in Figure 12.8. This fan draws air out through the rear brackets of the PC; it does not install into the bus, drawing its power instead from a branch of the power supply.

Figure 12.6

A Turbochip microprocessor upgrade in place on the Asus motherboard.

A heavier-duty slot fan is shown in Figure 12.9. This device projects deep into the case to draw air away from the CPU. The two fans can be articulated to direct their intake as close as possible to a source of heat.

Figure 12.7

Case fan.

Figure 12.8

Slot fan.

Figure 12.9

Dual-fan cooler.

13

A Tour of the Finished Machine

Our lowly demonstration PC has a new life: it has been equipped with a 366-MHz upgraded microprocessor, new memory, a set of USB ports, a new keyboard and mouse, and a USB screen camera. To the left of the system unit is an external CD-R that attaches to a new SCSI adapter.

On the screen, shown in Figure 13.1, the photo studio mascot cat Conch poses in an image captured with a digital camera.

Figure 13.2 shows a new machine built up from some of the components I've written about in this book. Based around the Abit BE6-II motherboard, this system includes a 500-MHz Pentium III microprocessor, 128 MB of SDRAM, a 20-GB hard drive, a multimedia video card in an AGP slot, a SCSI card, and an advanced sound card.

The modern case includes four cooling fans: one on the CPU, one on power supply, one in a bus slot, and an intake fan at the front.

Figure 13.1

The demonstration PC, fully upgraded.

Figure 13.2

An upgraded AGP motherboard with Pentium III microprocessor.

CHAPTER 14

Verifying and Configuring System Resources

All hardware devices need to have communication channels and memory addresses to exchange data and instructions with the system. In general, each device must establish and maintain its own identity. Conflicts between devices seeking to use the same memory address, interrupt, or DMA channel are the number one cause of crashes and errors on computers.

The basic system resources are:

- **I/O port address.** This is a specific physical location in the system memory that serves as the portal for the exchange of information between a device and the bus.

- **IRQ (interrupt request).** The device grabs the attention of the processor, or the processor of the device, by sending a wake-up call called an *interrupt*.

Figure 14.1

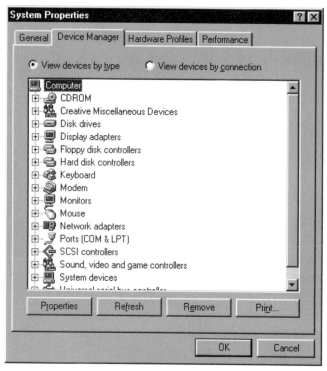

System Properties report.

Figure 14.2

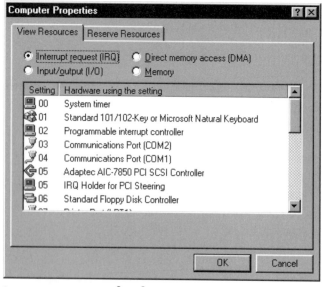

Interrupt request (IRQ) report.

■ **DMA (direct memory access) channel.** This is a pathway that allows the transfer of data in the system without having to go through the microprocessor itself.

Different types of devices have different requirements. Sound cards are among the most demanding in requiring an I/O address, an IRQ, and at least one DMA channel; some require more than one IRQ for advanced functions. Communications ports need an I/O address and IRQ.

In general, you cannot share I/O addresses. Under Windows 98 and plug-and-play systems, it is possible to share IRQs.

This chapter discusses conflicts and ways to avoid them.

1. Know the resources of the devices already in place in your system before you install a new device.

There are numerous ways to determine resources from within Windows. One is to go to Settings/Control Panel/System. Then click on the Device Manager tab. You'll see a System Properties screen like the one in Figure 14.1. Click on Computer. You'll see a Computer Properties screen with four radio buttons: interrupt request (IRQ), input/output (I/O), direct memory access (DMA), and memory. The results are shown in Figures 14.2, 14.3, 14.4, and 14.5.

Another way to obtain a report on system resources while running one of the Microsoft Office applications is to click on Help and then the About pulldown menu, for example, About Microsoft Word or About Microsoft Excel. Click on System Info. Two options are a detailed display of IRQ assignments, shown in Figure 14.6, and a display called Conflicts/Sharing shown in Figure 14.7, that shows which IRQs have more than one device assigned to them. Some systems may also have the DOS utility MSD.EXE, which provides much of the same information when run from the DOS prompt. Other third-party utilities also include system reports.

2. Determine the default settings for any new device you plan to install in the system. You can find this information in the specifications of the manual.

Devices that are not plug-and-play capable come with jumper or switch settings that are standard for the particular type of device. These are usually safe and appropriate, but the more devices you have in your system the more likely you are to run into conflicts.

Plug-and-play devices work with modern PCs and operating systems to automatically search for combinations of interrupts, DMA channels, and memory addresses that are not in conflict. In some systems you should be able to share some resources across particular classes of devices.

Figure 14.3

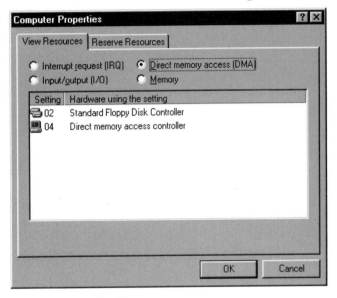

Input/output (I/O) report.

If you are upgrading an older system, look for adapters that offer a wide range of configuration options. Certain adapters can use "high IRQs"; these are resources numbered 9 and above.

3. Where possible, keep common adapters at their standard settings.

For example, don't change the memory or IRQ assignments for COM ports unless absolutely necessary because some software may attempt to deal with those locations directly instead of taking the extra step of letting the operating system look up the device name and checking to see if you have made any changes.

4. If your system behaves erratically, you may have resource conflicts.

Symptoms include system crashes and lockups, mouse freeze, devices not responding, distorted sound, and garbled characters on screen or errors in data transfer. Similar problems can also be caused by computer viruses. Be sure to install and use a virus checker regularly and search for viruses before making changes to system resources.

5. Under Windows 95/98, verify and correct settings under Device Manager.

Go to Settings/Control Panel/System/Device Manager. Click on the + to expand the subtree for various types of devices. You're looking for any

Figure 14.4

Direct memory access (DMA) report.

Figure 14.5

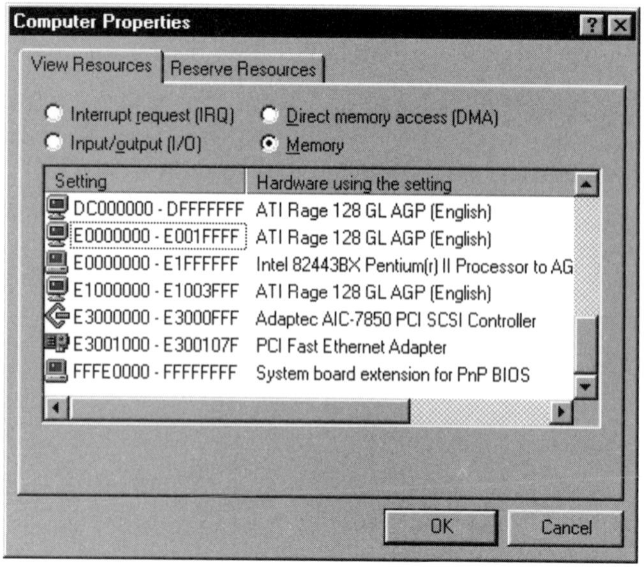

Memory report.

device marked by a yellow exclamation point or a red cross. A yellow exclamation point indicates a device that is a definite or potential source of conflict.

To investigate further or to make changes, double click on the device to open it. Then click on Resources. As shown in Figure 14.8, you'll see the current resources in use. In the lower half of the screen is a list of conflicting devices.

If you have a conflict or want to change the assignment of a working device to make room for another device, unclick the Use Automatic Settings check box.

To make a change, highlight one of the resource types, and then click on Change Setting. If you receive the message, "This resource setting cannot be modified," the current configuration does not allow changes. Try selecting a different basic configuration and try again; click on Change Setting until you see an Edit screen for the resource.

For example, in Figure 14.9, the Edit Interrupt Request allows you to choose from all of the IRQs available to devices. If you choose an IRQ that will cause a conflict, the Conflict information screen informs you of this and tells you the identity of the other device using the same resource. You can choose to search for a non-conflicting resource, or you can accept a conflict and make changes elsewhere.

Once you have completed the changes, you'll need to reboot the system to allow them to take effect. After the machine is up and running, return to the Control Panel and Systems display and search for exclamation points.

Figure 14.6

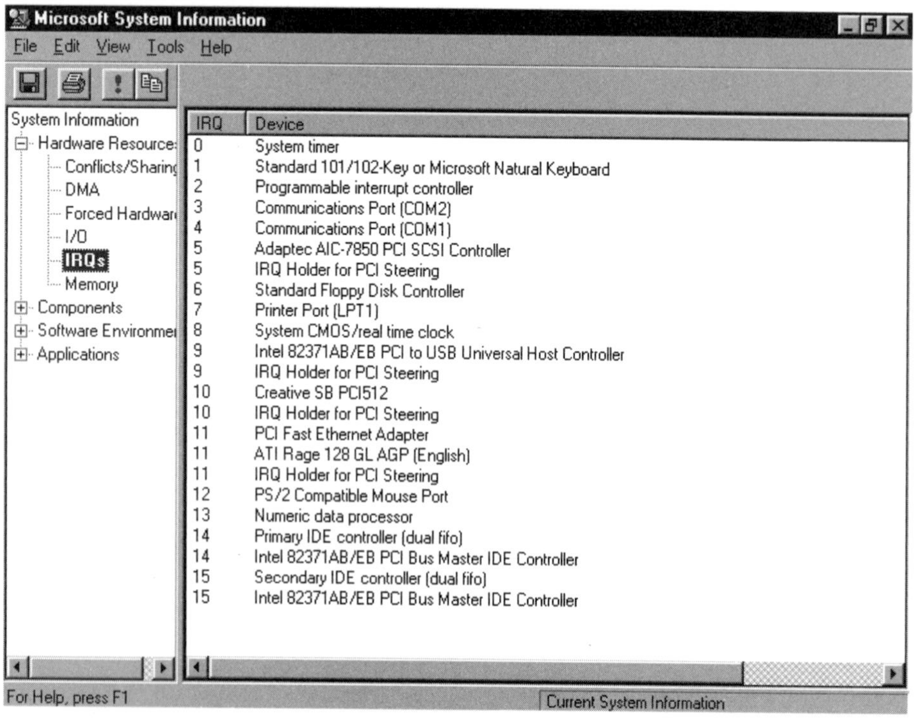

System Info from within Microsoft applications.

The red cross indicates a device that has been disabled. In most cases, this indicates a device that the user has specifically instructed Windows to exclude from the current profile. Doing so frees up system resources that would ordinarily be claimed by the device. If you find a device disabled that should instead be available to you, click on the device and instruct Windows to include it in the current profile; you'll have to reboot for the change to take effect.

Figure 14.7

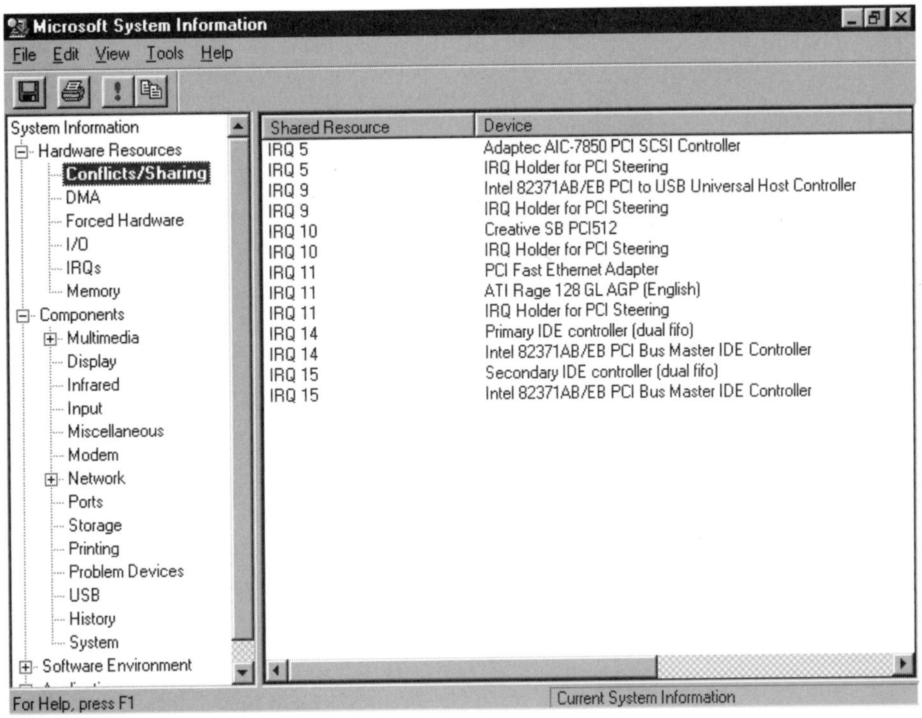

Conflicts/sharing report.

Figure 14.8

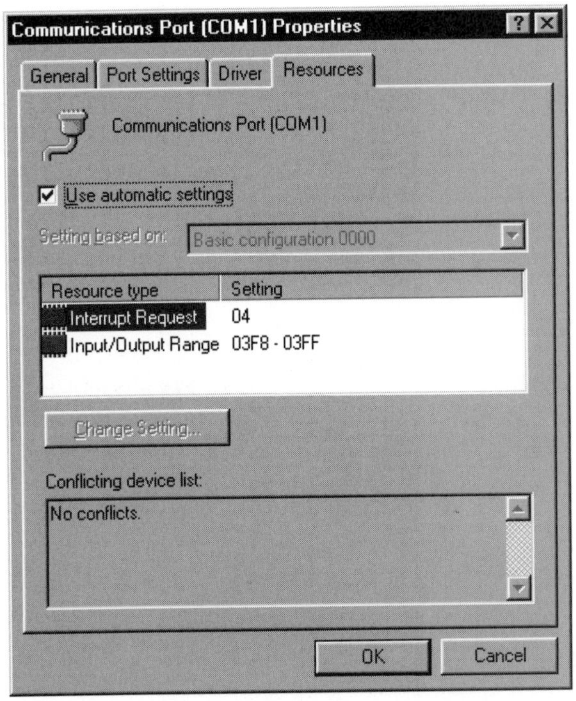

Resources report from Device Manager.

Figure 14.9

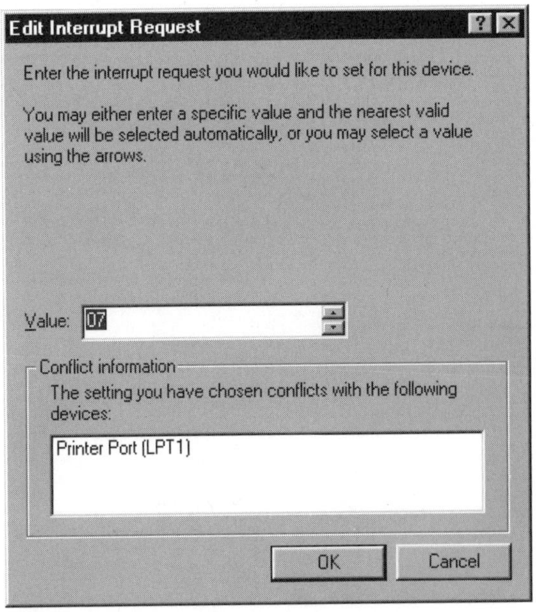

Edit Interrupt Request screen.

Appendix 1
Standard Serial Port Resources

Name	IRQ	I/O Address
COM1	IRQ4	3F8
COM2	IRQ3	2F8
COM3	IRQ4	3E8
COM4	IRQ3	2E8
COM5	IRQ4	3E0
COM6	IRQ3	2E0
COM7	IRQ4	338
COM8	IRQ3	238

Appendix 2
Standard Parallel Port Resources

Name	IRQ	I/O Address
LPT1	IRQ7	3BCh or 378h
LPT2	IRQ5	378h or 278h
LPT3		278h

Modern Pentium-class computers support 16 IRQs; of those, 4 are reserved for system devices, leaving 12 available for allocation to adapters and other devices.

Appendix 3
Standard Interrupt Requests (IRQs)

IRQ	Standard Function	Card Type
0	Timer clock	System device
1	Keyboard	System device
2	Second IRQ cascade*	System device
3	Serial port 2 (COM2, COM4)	8/16 bits
4	Serial port 1 (COM1, COM3)	8/16 bits
5	Sound card/parallel port 2 (LPT2)	8/16 bits
6	Floppy disk controller	8/16 bits
7	Parallel port 1 (LPT1)	8/16 bits
8	Real-time clock	System device
9	Redirected from IRQ2*	8/16 bits
10	Available	16 bits
11	Available	16 bits
12	Available/PS/2 mouse	16 bits
13	Math coprocessor	System device
14	Primary IDE HDD	16 bits
15	Available/secondary IDE HDD	16 bits

Appendix 4
Direct Memory Access (DMA)

DMA	Standard Function	Transfer
0	Available	8 bits
1	Available/sound card	8 bits
2	Floppy disk controller	8 bits
3	Available	8 bits
4	First DMA controller cascade	System device
5	Available/sound card	16 bits
6	Available	16 bits
7	Available	16 bits

IRQ2 is a portal to IRQ9 and higher.

index

Note: Boldface numbers indicate illustrations.